MW01198774

BLUEPRINT for Your LIBRARY MARKETING PLAN

A Guide to Help You Survive and Thrive

PATRICIA H. FISHER   MARSEILLE M. PRIDE

With assistance from
Ellen G. Miller

AMERICAN LIBRARY ASSOCIATION

Chicago   2006

While extensive effort has gone into ensuring the reliability of information appearing in this book, the publisher makes no warranty, express or implied, on the accuracy or reliability of the information, and does not assume and hereby disclaims any liability to any person for any loss or damage caused by errors or omissions in this publication.

Design and composition by ALA Editions in Minion and Univers using QuarkXPress 5.0 on a PC platform.

Printed on 5-pound white offset, a pH-neutral stock, and bound in 10-point cover stock by

The paper used in this publication meets the minimum requirements of American National Standard for Information Sciences—Permanence of Paper for Printed Library Materials, ANSI Z39.48-1992. ∞

Library of Congress Cataloging-in-Publication Data

Fisher, Patricia H. (Patricia Holts)
    Blueprint for your library marketing plan : a guide to help you survive and thrive / by Patricia H. Fisher and Marseille M. Pride ; with assistance from Ellen G. Miller.
       p. cm.
    Includes bibliographical references and index.
    ISBN 0-8389-0909-4
    1. Libraries—United States—Marketing. 2. Libraries—Public relations—United States. 3. Library planning—United States. 4. Strategic planning—United States. I. Pride, Marseille M. (Marseille Miles) II. Miller, Ellen G. III. Title.
    Z716.3.F57 2005
    021.7—dc22   2005015016

Printed in the United States of America

10 09 08 07 06   5 4 3 2 1

CONTENTS

MARKETING PLAN WORKSHEETS

Marketing Plan Worksheets are also available at www.ala.org/editions/extras/Fisher09096

FIGURES

PREFACE

The only way to predict the future is to create it.

—Ray Falcione

Marketing is about bringing them in and bringing them back. The competition understands this and pursues repeat business. Librarians can no longer afford to leave getting repeat customers to either chance or goodwill. Libraries are in danger of becoming irrelevant relics rather than the key players in the New World order that we believe they should be. Marketing is a stance and an attitude that focuses on meeting the needs of users. Marketing is a means of ensuring that libraries, librarians, and librarianship are integrated into both today's and tomorrow's emerging global culture. Marketing is not separate from good practice. It is good practice. Some librarians already know many of the steps needed to take a marketing approach to library operations and services.

Library literature over the past fifteen to twenty years has numerous entries on the benefits of using a marketing approach in the delivery of library services. But many of these articles focus on the promotions and public relations aspects of the process and in so doing tend to miss the forest for the trees. Many librarians do not realize that marketing touches every aspect of delivering library service; they are performing marketing functions without realizing it.

ABOUT THIS BOOK

Competition for your community's support, funding, and resources is at an all-time high, and there is no end in sight. A major premise of this book is that developing and following a well-considered marketing plan enables your library to come out ahead in the competition—not just to survive, but to thrive. With the aid of a set of worksheets you individualize, this book guides you through the process of writing a marketing plan that is substantive and useful. With a completed plan, you will be able to present a more compelling case to funding agencies and to operate in a more strategic fashion. A well-designed and well-executed marketing plan is, in a sense, a map and a compass. You may be able to arrive at your desired destination without them, but using these items helps you arrive in a more efficient and expeditious manner.

If you are currently engaged in any aspect of marketing library services, using the worksheets may provide you a frame and a window to evaluate your process. It is best to focus on only one or two services to get the process under your belt, then you can branch out to other services. Although you may choose not to use all of the worksheets or complete those you use in great detail, it is advisable to review them completely.

The authors are uniquely qualified to address marketing and libraries. Pat Fisher has more than twenty years of marketing experience from the private sector. She has served as a public library trustee for more than ten years and is currently the principal of P. Fisher and Associates, a library consulting firm with specialties in marketing, strategic planning, advocacy, and public relations. Marcy Pride has more than twenty years of public relations experience in the corporate, private, and public sectors. Additionally, Ms. Pride has worked in public, academic, and special libraries—and in both public services and technical services. In 2002 her project "Maryland Public Libraries, It's Never Too Early" won a John Cotton Dana Award. Ellen Miller is president of the Ellen Miller Group, a company that specializes in positioning strategies for complex public and for-profit organizations. She has worked as a librarian in academic libraries and has more than twenty-five years of experience as a public library trustee. This book blends the authors' knowledge and experience to provide you with a practical, straightforward approach to developing a marketing plan for your services.

HOW THIS BOOK IS ORGANIZED

The first two chapters of *Blueprint for Your Library Marketing Plan* offer preliminaries and the next eight chapters help you with development of a marketing plan. The ten chapters each begin with a list of chapter objectives and a vignette to demonstrate the concept and part of the marketing plan covered in the chapter. The chapters also include one or more illustrations of libraries applying the concept and conclude with Quick-Start Tips as summary reminders.

An important feature of this book is the set of Marketing Plan Worksheets—forms you can use to build a detailed marketing plan for your specific services and circumstances. The use of each worksheet is explained in detail in the appropriate chapter; all worksheets are gathered at the back of the book and may be photocopied for use in the design and completion of your marketing plans. It is best to complete these forms as you go. If developing your marketing plan is part of a committee process, each committee member could complete individual copies of forms and then consensus could determine the final outcome. When using the worksheets, it is not necessary to spend a huge amount of time collecting data. Use the data you have, extrapolate when you can, and make educated guesses when you need to. Remember, though: As you complete the forms, you are completing your marketing plan.

A relatively new library service, chat reference, is used throughout the book as a model to illustrate the development of a marketing plan. Since this service is currently being offered by public libraries, academic libraries, and partnerships between these and school libraries, we believe it is a suitable choice for a model.

> *Chapter 1* focuses on your strategic plan and its significance to your marketing efforts. It is an important foundational piece in the development of your marketing plan.
>
> *Chapter 2* is about gathering data to help you determine whom it is you are serving, what their needs are now, and what they are likely to need or want in the future.
>
> *Chapter 3* defines marketing and describes the marketing plan in detail.

Chapter 4 deals with defining the elements that make up your service and discusses the relevance of partnerships to supplement resources needed to deliver your services.

Chapter 5 covers target markets and how to define their needs.

Chapter 6 looks at how your services, your positioning, your brand, and your image compare to others in the market.

Chapter 7 discusses setting goals and objectives and the levels of marketing strategy, including the market mix.

Chapter 8 focuses on promotion and its place in the marketing plan, including advertising, public relations, and uses of various promotional strategies.

Chapter 9 deals with tactics, strategic budgets, and development of controls for overall tracking and implementation of the marketing plan.

Chapter 10 provides instruction on how to develop a summary of your marketing plan. The need to determine how you will evaluate your marketing efforts is also discussed.

As you progress through the book, you will gain an increased sense of control and a greater understanding of how to speak the language of the users of your services.

To keep up with new marketing ideas and remain current, we suggest the websites below as good places to begin.

American Library Association, "@ your library" campaign: http://www.ala.org/alas/pio/campaign/campaignamericas.htm, for campaign news, tools, and resources.

3M: http://cms.3m.com/cms/US/en/2-115/czrRzFZ/view.jhtml, for materials to help academic and research librarians search for a tool set and a process for creating a library marketing plan and promotional campaign.

Thompson Gale Publishing, Market Your Library: http://www.gale.com/free_resources/marketing/index.htm, for free resources (guidelines and simple-to-use templates) to help promote public and specialized libraries.

Chris Olson's Marketing Treasures: http://www.chrisolson.com/marketingtreasures/mtresources.html, a monthly newsletter source of promotion ideas, marketing insights, and resources.

P. Fisher and Associates: http://www.pfisherassociates.com/whatwedo/marketing.html, a source of marketing tips and highlights of marketing workshops.

If at any time you want feedback on your process, or you want to share your successes, feel free to contact P. Fisher and Associates at pat@pfisherassociates.com, using "Blueprint for Your Library Marketing Plan" in the subject line. We hope you will keep in touch.

ACKNOWLEDGMENTS

Many thanks to our friends and colleagues, both in and out of libraryland, who have shared your experiences, thoughts, and questions about marketing with us. There is always something new to learn and we have learned a great deal from all of you.

We would especially like to thank Joe Thompson and the Maryland AskUsNow! virtual reference consortium. Joe shared with us the team's early experiences developing the chat reference service, which provided us several quotes for this book and gave us a basis for developing the fictional chat reference examples we used to explain several marketing concepts. We congratulate the Maryland AskUsNow! consortium (nineteen public libraries, five academic libraries, and the Maryland State Law Library) for winning an Exemplary Service Award at the 2004 Virtual Reference Desk Conference in Cincinnati, Ohio.

Thanks to our editors, Lindsay Harmon, Emily Moroni, and John Thomas, for their patience and expertise in making this a readable and useful tool for librarians.

Special thanks and appreciation to our extraordinarily patient spouses, Ron Fisher Sr. and Melvin Pride, who encouraged us to keep working to finish this workbook when we were ready to give up.

one

Strategic Plans

Dust Catchers or Power Tools
for Your Marketing Plan?

There is nothing more difficult to take in hand, more perilous to conduct, or more uncertain in success, than to take the lead in the introduction of a new order of things.

—Niccolo Machiavelli, *The Prince*

chapter objectives

1. Grade your strategic plan. Is it ready to use in marketing?

2. Identify quick fixes for your current strategic plan, if needed.

3. Learn how other libraries have used their strategic plan in marketing areas such as customer service and visibility.

The library faculty at Mississippi State University wanted a more central presence on campus. They included this as a goal in their strategic plan and set out to design opportunities to shine. Enter Gail Peyton, outreach librarian par excellence, and life has never been the same! Wherever you go, you're reminded of library services. Library faculty publish and present at astounding rates; students take notes when librarians interact with them at the reference desk and seek out librarians for individual consultations. Did this happen by accident? Of course not. Was it good luck? Maybe in part, but mostly it happened by planning the work and working the plan—the strategic plan, that is.[1]

Inherent in Mississippi State University's strategic plan is a hint of an additional plan that addresses marketing promotional strategies and tactics. If you want to follow this example, your first step is to have a strategic plan that states your goals and provides you with a blueprint of strategies, tactics, and additional plans to achieve your goals, one of which is your marketing plan.

THE STRATEGIC PLAN

Ensure success in establishing your library's "new order" by getting the most out of your current strategic plan or developing a new one. Show elected officials, academic administrators, voters, and other decision makers that your library is a central presence in the community or on your campus. This will lead stakeholders to see the wisdom of protecting or even growing your budget. Why? Because the content of your strategic plan, methods, visions, goals, objectives, and strategies and the companion marketing plan mirror expressed community needs. "City councils and county commissions don't usually worry about the plan's contents, but they want to know your process," says Dr. Martha Hale, dean of Catholic University's School of Library and Information Science. "When the librarian discusses which demographic group is growing fastest, he/she becomes the expert. It shows that your library's services are matching needs."[2] Showing your expertise helps get your library to the decision-making table instead of waiting for crumbs to drop off.

Some libraries do strategic planning because somebody required it. For public libraries, that somebody can be the library board, state library, regional/cooperative system, city, township, or county. For academic libraries, the college may be gearing up for accreditation review . . . or for budget cuts.

Others write strategic plans because they are part of modern librarianship. Leading a strategic planning process gives deans and directors success in gaining buy-in from boards, faculty members, students, community members, and staff as they develop a common cause. They can use that expertise when bargaining for more resources . . . and when looking for a new job.

No matter why your library created its strategic plan, the question is, are you getting adequate return on that investment (ROI) of time and dollars? Staff spent many hours in-house doing research, filling out forms, and preparing reports. Community members and perhaps members of your friends groups participated in focus groups and meetings or filled out surveys. If you hired an outside facilitator, that person's consulting fee and travel costs should be included in your calculation of time and money spent on strategic planning.

Altogether, your strategic planning process could cost your library several thousand dollars. Those who fund you, especially taxpayers, expect their dollars to be used wisely. They don't expect your strategic plan to gather dust on a shelf. Not getting the most from your strategic plan is like buying a full-featured luxury car . . . and then putting it up on blocks in the garage for fear of scratches. You've wasted money and time.

EVALUATING THE STRATEGIC PLAN: WHAT'S YOUR GRADE ON ROI?

Getting ROI starts with evaluating your plan. Pull it off that shelf. Have a team review its contents and its planning process. Does it have gaps? If so, they should be fixed before you start marketing planning. Your strategic plan is your organization's overall blueprint for the future. It must be strong if you want an effective marketing plan. The strategic planning process has five phases, which you should grade. You can use worksheet 1, the Strategic Planning Self-Grade Card, to grade your plan. It lists the phases and suggests questions you should ask yourself about the motivation behind the plan and about its contents, uses, and effectiveness. Use a grading scale of A for Excellent and F for Failure.

Phase 1: Starting Up. Review the reasons you are embarking on a process to develop or update your strategic plan. These may determine your timetable, your planning budget, or your choice of in-house or outside facilitator. Determine the "ground rules" for decision making and handling other tough topics up front.

Phase 2: The Planning Process. Plans rise or fall on their methodology. If only the director/dean and managers are on the planning team, you'll forfeit claims for community or stakeholder involvement. If you skimp on needed data categories such as demographic, behavioral (library usage), psychographic, and library resources (discussed in chapter 2), you'll jeopardize your findings and therefore your conclusions.

Phase 3: The Plan's Contents. There are many strategic planning models that prescribe process and content for public and academic libraries. Public libraries often turn to Sandra Nelson's *The New Planning for Results*, prepared for the Public Library Association.[3] Academic libraries may follow the ACRL standard or the example of a specific institution such as the University of Arizona. Others might consult key journals such as *Library Journal*, *Public Management*, *Academic Libraries*, *Library Trends*, or the *Harvard Business Review*, which routinely include articles on strategic planning.[4] And some deans/directors rely on their facilitator for a planning model combining elements of several models. For example, Ellen Miller used a business model with busy library boards paired with a staff assessment of how well they were carrying out thirteen service responses listed in *The New Planning for Results*.[5] Whichever planning model you choose, common document elements include vision, mission, service responses (if using *The New Planning for Results*), and values along with goals and objectives. How do you make your plan concrete? Some planners use quantifiable objectives with due date, responsible person, and so forth. Others create a companion action plan, also known as a business plan or annual work plan, for each fiscal year budget, showing specific steps to be taken, resources needed, due date, and responsible person. One of these steps may be to create a marketing plan for key library services.

Phase 4: Status, Review, and Update. Too often ignored, evaluation determines the ROI of all those hours and dollars. Start with regular status reviews by the managers and governance body. Then decide when the next planning cycle starts. Finally, consider adding implementation of the strategic plan to the annual performance review of your managers—it'll get them to pull the plan off that shelf!

Phase 5: Implementation. From collection development to marketing, many companion plans depend on the "umbrella" strategic plan. These supporting plans provide major returns on your investment.

Using worksheet 1, what grades did you assign? If your plan got more than two Ds and four Fs, fix those gaps before proceeding in this book. Use figure 1-1 for fast, practical fixes. Once your plan is shipshape, it's time to implement.

FIGURE 1-1
Fix-It Tool Kit

Gaps Needing Fixing	Possible Steps	Desired Outcomes
Poor Start-Up 1. Inadequate amount of time allotted to develop the plan 2. Unrealistic budget allotted for planning 3. Inadequate or no ground rules set for decision making and handling tough topics 4. Poor choice of facilitator	At a managers' meeting, review lessons learned about the start-up process; determine how to apply those lessons to future planning efforts.	Better start-up on future planning projects (strategic plans, marketing plans, etc.)
Flawed Planning Process 1. Poor community participation 2. Poor data 3. Poor director/dean support	1. Take plan to many outside groups for input. 2. Get new data for areas with least data. 3. At managers' meeting, discuss the year's priorities.	1. Revised plan; publicity of changes and of those who helped 2. Revised plan with usable, defendable data 3. Improved director/dean support for marketing planning
Inadequate Content 1. Doesn't meet requirements 2. Too few mandatory sections (vision, values, mission statement, goals/objectives)	1. Decide on stopgap fixes until next planning cycle. 2. If no vision, restart strategic planning. 3. If no mission or values, add now.	1. Smaller but usable plan 2. Brand-new strategic plan 3. Revised plan with mission and values
Poor Implementation 1. Sits on a shelf or in a file cabinet 2. Ignored when making departmental goals 3. Poor stakeholder awareness of plan or process 4. Ignored as a guide for marketing	1. Show administration how plan can help get more library resources. 2. Show administration how plan can bring departments closer. 3. Show administration how plan can help get positive recognition from stakeholders and decision makers. 4. Show administration the steps to create a marketing plan.	1. Plan used to support efforts to obtain more resources and defend against cuts 2. Department heads required to cite the plan for unit goals 3. Publicity generated about the plan and its process 4. Marketing plan made consistent with strategic plan
No or Little Evaluation 1. Poor or no review of the plan 2. No update planned	1. Put on managers' meeting agenda. 2. Put on managers' meeting agenda.	1. Decide on a date for next review. 2. Decide on an update schedule.

HOW LIBRARIES USE STRATEGIC PLANS

Are you worried that one of your board members or department heads will balk at strategic planning "just" to create a marketing plan? Then point out these five additional uses.

1. Fighting Threats to Library Standards and Budgets

In the fall of 2002, lower than expected student enrollment prompted budget cuts at Indiana's Goshen College, including dropping some academic programs. In spite of this, the Harold and Wilma Good Library received few cuts. Why? The library director credits its strategic planning process, which included input from many campus stakeholder groups as well as peer institution comparisons.

"The strategic planning process gave us data that proved effective in our efforts to minimize staff reductions and fend off even deeper budget cuts," said director Lisa Guedea Carreno. "Student and faculty surveys and focus groups yielded convincing evidence that many on campus still rely on the library very heavily. High-level administrators were asked how the library could contribute to student recruitment and retention. Their responses came in very handy when, several months later, some of these very same administrators asked me to consider cutting library hours, staff and services that students had recently identified as important elements of their academic success."[6]

2. Allocating Scarce Dollars, Space, and People

It's simple. To get the plan carried out in daily operations, departmental budget requests must reflect it. Early in 2003, the University of Notre Dame's Edward H. Arnold University Libraries finished its strategic plan. "We intend to use it as a framework for departmental goals and objectives," stated library director Jennifer Younger. "We would like each department to link its goals to specific directions and initiatives in our strategic plan. We know the plan isn't perfect, so if we find gaps identified by departmental goals, we will adjust the plan."[7]

3. Advocating for More Dollars, Staff, Space, and Hours

Sooner or later, virtually all libraries need more resources. Chestatee Regional Library System serves two county libraries in southwestern Georgia. In 1999 a broad-based committee of staff, members of the community, and trustees brought in Sandra Nelson, author of PLA's *The New Planning for Results*.

"Our strategic plan is a great communication tool and it helps convince funders and the general community that we are spending tax dollars wisely," said director Lyn Hopper. A follow-up step, called for in the strategic plan, was to create an external communications plan, which recommended eight methods of communication. One of the eight methods cited is the director's advocacy list, an as-needed broadcast e-mail informing the community about key topics or asking for political action.[8]

4. Establishing Branding and Positioning Strategies

Just as companies seek to establish their name, products, and image positively with selected target markets, libraries need to do the same thing. The Strengths, Weaknesses, Opportunities, and Threats (SWOT) analysis section of the strategic plan provides excellent insight about how your library is viewed by your target markets.

You should understand the difference between branding and its sibling—positioning. Branding seeks to establish an emotional attachment; it depends on recognition. In contrast, positioning demonstrates the true and identifiable value of a product or service to a specific target market. See more on branding and positioning in chapter 6.

Branding can be jump-started by coordinating your plan with your parent university, city, or county. Take advantage of its name and logo recognition among target markets. "We linked our plan to the campus plan, so the priorities we identify also fit within the campus priorities of student success, faculty and staff excellence, community partnerships and economic development in the Calumet Region," stated Kathryn Carpenter, dean of Purdue University–Calumet, which serves about 9,000 students in northwestern Indiana.[9]

Positioning requires you to analyze how your target markets view your library services compared to competitive alternatives. Let your strategic plan help you determine markets to target for a specific service. As part of your marketing plan, analyze competing alternatives and service providers. Determine your service's position compared to the competition; are your services easier to use, faster with results, more helpful, less expensive?

5. Recruiting Top-Quality Board Members

Whether elected or appointed, whether advisory or decision-making, it's hard to get good trustees. Getting positive media coverage during and after planning, however, shows business know-how. This, coupled with one-on-one recruitment by a current trustee wielding your strategic plan, shows that your library board is on the move. Everybody wants to be part of an organization on the move.

Marjorie Flowers serves ten libraries in the Green River/Pennyrile regional office of the Kentucky Department of Libraries, based in Owensboro. She is also acting head of the Northern Kentucky region, consisting of ten counties. "One of the selling points of getting counties to do [strategic planning] is that it's a wonderful recruitment tool for new board members," Flowers stated. "When you go through the process of selecting community members for the planning committee, you come up with people you didn't necessarily know about before."[10]

STRATEGIC PLANNING VS. MARKETING PLANNING

There are several companion plans to a strategic plan, such as the marketing plan, capital improvement plan, advocacy plan, and collection development plan. In this book, we provide a blueprint for developing the marketing plan and discuss the relationship of the plans. So how does the marketing plan relate to the strategic plan?

Unlike the chicken and the egg, we know that a strategic plan comes first. It is the blueprint that shows the difference your library seeks to make in the lives of its stakeholders. Your strategic plan identifies *ends*, whereas its companion marketing plan deals with *means*. Figure 1-2 shows the relationship between the two.

Using the Strategic Plan for Marketing

Public and academic libraries knowingly and unknowingly use their strategic plans to launch marketing activities. Some librarians call it *outreach* (reaching out to diverse communities). In marketing parlance it's called *selecting and analyzing target markets*.

FIGURE 1-2
Relationship between Marketing and Strategic Planning

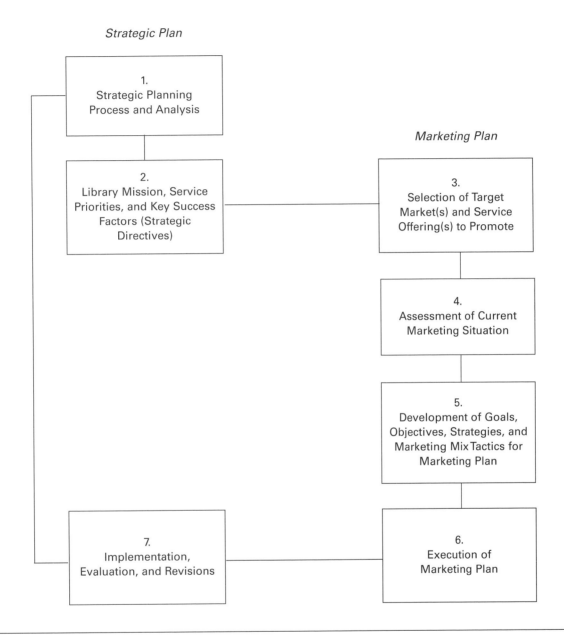

Strategic Plan

1.
Strategic Planning
Process and Analysis

Marketing Plan

2.
Library Mission, Service
Priorities, and Key Success
Factors (Strategic
Directives)

3.
Selection of Target
Market(s) and Service
Offering(s) to Promote

4.
Assessment of Current
Marketing Situation

5.
Development of Goals,
Objectives, Strategies, and
Marketing Mix Tactics for
Marketing Plan

7.
Implementation,
Evaluation, and Revisions

6.
Execution of
Marketing Plan

OUTREACH TO SERVICE PROVIDERS

During its strategic planning process, the Morrisson-Reeves Library of Richmond, which serves a population of 73,000 in extreme eastern Indiana, established a goal to increase visibility in the community. One focus group with service providers to special populations and another group with literacy providers revealed a lack of awareness about some services and programs.

"Caregivers of the homebound didn't know we offered home delivery," said director Carol B. Smyth. "Now we are marketing the library to them and their clientele in a different way. One thing that stood out [with literacy providers] was how we all were doing something in common, but there was a duplication of effort," Smyth noted. "We need to improve letting them know what we're doing and what we have to offer. And we need to find out what they are doing."[11]

OUTREACH TO CHILDREN

For one Kentucky library, strengthening children's services emerged as a top priority in 1999. The sixteen-person planning committee included community members. They used *The New Planning for Results* model. "During a discussion conducted at one of the planning sessions, it became clear that we needed to improve our outreach services for children," said Deborah Mesplay, director of the Daviess County Public Library. "We identified all day care centers, Head Starts, and nursery schools serving kids under five years of age. Letters went to them describing services such as presenting story hour at their facility. When fifteen centers responded positively, a full-time employee was assigned to this outreach program. Soon she had little time for other duties as the number of agencies seeking help grew every year." When asked about the results of the outreach effort, Mesplay responded, "We have exceeded our goal. Over three years, the annual target was to reach at least 25 percent of the county's estimated 6,133 children under five. At the end of three years, we had in fact reached 30 percent of the children in that age group." Today, a staff member working 25–30 hours/week provides outreach services to that group.[12]

Informal marketing methods to reach target markets are rooted in many library strategic plans. Other benefits of using a strategic plan for marketing include these:

- Updating current practices, programs, and services
- Rethinking data gathered and how it's used
- Linking departments more closely because their goals support the plan
- Getting your team familiar with the structure and discipline needed for marketing planning
- Allocating scarce resources

DOES MARKET SEGMENTATION FOSTER INEQUALITY?

Allocating more resources to special groups targeted for outreach poses problems for some in the library profession. Philosophically, the library profession is committed to equality of information access for all. That concept is especially strong for tax-supported entities. Public, academic, school, and special libraries work hard to help assure that no person is left out. Cooperative devices such as union catalogs, web hot links, and reciprocal borrowing privileges all demonstrate this commitment. As an industry, libraries do everything possible to serve everyone in the best possible way, from homeschoolers to the homebound. But there's a catch: When all services and programs are equally important, all are of the highest priority. All get an equal, albeit meager, share of the available resources.

Marketing planning puts a different spin on equality. Market segmentation analysis gives you the tools to select a few markets on which to focus your efforts. Why? Because there are never enough resources to go around. Setting priorities is a must. Marketers believe it is better to serve a few markets well than serve all markets poorly. Fortunately, your strategic plan helps you implement market segmentation. It establishes good reasons for deciding that some things come first and therefore get more money, staff, space, or equipment. That's where a representative planning team pays off politically: It wasn't just the dean/director or managers who decided to upgrade one program or cut funds to another.

CONCLUSION

Strategic planning makes sense *only* if you're going to use it. Otherwise, it's a waste of precious taxpayer dollars, staff time, and library space and equipment. On the bright side, finishing your plan means the hard work is over. Now it's time to get some ROI and have fun brainstorming about your marketing plan.

quick-start tips

What comes first? Your strategic plan. It sets the foundation for marketing planning. But is your strategic plan good enough? Here's how to find out:

1. Pull out your current strategic plan. Refresh your memory about its process and contents.

2. Using worksheet 1, grade its five phases: starting up, planning process, plan's contents, evaluation, and implementation. Does it meet modern strategic planning criteria? For example, were staff and community stakeholders involved in the process, not just the board and director? Does the plan include these essential sections:

   Vision—the difference the library seeks to make in the lives of those it serves

   Values—the unchanging norms that define how staff and customers behave toward each other

   Mission statement—the library's purpose and who is benefited

   Goals and objectives (sometimes called outcomes and strategies)—actions that will help achieve the library's vision

   For posterity, does it include a description of the methodology used? Does it have a list of the planning team members and their affiliations? It is helpful to show that not just a group of library staff sat around and dreamed up ways to spend taxpayer dollars. And is there a companion annual action plan—something to show the steps to be taken in the upcoming fiscal year, including who's responsible and target start and finish dates?

   Assign each of the items a grade (A, B, C, D, or F). If you have more than four Fs and two Ds, go to step 3. Why? Because your library isn't ready for marketing planning yet. If your grades are higher, go to step 4.

3. Use figure 1-1, the Fix-It Tool Kit, for practical quick fixes to your strategic plan.

4. Proceed to chapter 2 of this book.

NOTES

1. Gail Peyton, telephone interview, May 3, 2004.
2. Martha Hale, telephone interview, February 24, 2003.
3. Sandra Nelson, for the Public Library Association, *The New Planning for Results* (Chicago: American Library Association, 2001).

4. For example, Herbert S. White, "Planning and Evaluation: The Endless Carousel," *Library Journal* 122 (November 15): 38–41; Vicki Ray, "From Strategic Planning to Visioning: Tools for Navigating the Future," *Public Management* 83 (May 2000): 4–9; or John N. Berry III, "Arizona's New Model: An Academic Library for the Present and the Future," *Academic Libraries* 127 (November 1, 2002): 40–42.

5. Ellen G. Miller, "Strategic Positioning: Planning to Achieve Your Library's Vision," *Indiana Libraries* 17 (November 1998): 3–7.

6. Lisa Guedea Carreno, e-mail, March 3, 2003.

7. Jennifer Younger, e-mail, February 19, 2003.

8. Lyn Hopper, e-mail, February 20, 2003.

9. Kathryn Carpenter, e-mail, February 20, 2003.

10. Marjorie Flowers, telephone interview, February 28, 2003.

11. Carol B. Smyth, telephone interview, February 24, 2003.

12. Deborah Mesplay, telephone interview, February 28, 2003.

two

Mining Data
Discovering Trends

Paying attention to trends not only provides insight into how tomorrow will be, it can also wake us up to an existing condition of which we are not yet aware.

—Darlene Weingand, *Future-Driven Library Marketing*

chapter objectives

1. Provide insight into how demographic, behavioral, and psychographic data can be useful in developing goals, strategies, and tactics of a marketing plan.

2. Define and describe trends, trend analysis, demographics, behavioral data, and psychographics.

3. Introduce data collection worksheets and suggest sources of data.

4. Provide sample models and worksheets for looking at trends and drawing conclusions.

5. List possible trends to monitor.

6. Provide data on the customer universe needed to select one or more target markets for a specific product or service.

Late in 1999, Ohio's Lakewood Public Library recognized it had a problem or, more aptly, a challenge: after running some studies on its service area, it discovered that one of its biggest subsets of residents was hardly using the library. "Many people had a perception of Lakewood as being a city of families and senior citizens," said John Guscott, the library's manager of electronic services. "Our experiences at the library over the past few years suggested otherwise—that it was fast becoming a city dominated by young, professional (but non-mainstream) singles."

Working with the PRIZM lifestyle segmentation system created by California marketing research firm Claritas, Guscott prepared a marketing report that divided the residents in the Lakewood library service area into nine clusters, ranked by size. He discovered that the largest cluster— "Urban Achievers," representing 14,433 residents (nearly 26 percent of the total population in the service area)—was not using the library. He also compiled specific information about the Urban Achievers' ethnicity, age range, level of education, type of employment (e.g., "white collar/professional"), type of housing (rent or own), median income, median home value, key issues ("gay rights or environmental protection"), and politics (e.g., "liberal independent"). The most intriguing part of the cluster profile and the one that provided the most insight into each cluster's general consumer tastes was the PRIZM section titled "Consumer Pattern." Here the first group and largest cluster, Urban Achievers, was characterized as "behaving like middle-class sophisticates" and gravitating toward a welter of consumer outlets, products, and brands, including "specialty shops, ethnic markets, family restaurants, delis, sushi bars, taco joints, Nordstrom, jazz music, Kias, Volkswagens, and Nissans." Their composite "interests" were also telling: "multiculturalism, intellectually challenging pursuits, theater, adult education, libraries, public broadcasting and alternative health." Reflecting on the data gathered about the clusters, Guscott said, "Then we took it to the next step and figured out the programming and content that would attract them [Urban Achievers] to the library."[1]

Before Lakewood Public Library could prepare a plan to develop the products and services (programming and content) that would attract their target markets to the library, they had to gather data about the composition, needs, and interests of those markets. This step is often referred to as *pre-planning*.

PRE-PLANNING

The first step in planning, whether strategic or marketing, requires gathering information from many sources. Fortunately for you, information is a librarian's specialty. Marketing plans use a lot of the information you have already gathered for your strategic plan. Your task is to zoom in on only the information relevant to the products or services you intend to promote. The categories of information needed are statistics and trends related to your community/campus, your product/service, your chosen target market (this chapter and chapter 5), and competitive alternatives to your product/service (chapter 6).

Observing the trends regarding the age and family composition of residents in the Lakewood Public Library serving area pointed out the need for more demographic research. Trends that can affect the services libraries offer can be discovered by observation and by analyzing demographic and behavioral data (library usage) compiled for your strategic plan. Worksheets provided at the back of this book can be used to record the information you gather or excerpt from your strategic plan.

Making observations and gathering information may be a shared activity for members of a marketing planning team. This same team can take on the brainstorming necessary to make assumptions to fill in the gaps of unobtainable information, set the marketing objectives and goals, and develop the strategies and tactics to achieve the objectives and goals of your plan.

What Are Trends?

Trends are about change. The change could occur in either the external (in the community) or the internal (in the library) environment. You might see a change in the number of preschool children in the community; a change in expectations of college students regarding speed and delivery of responses to reference questions; a change in user attitudes about relying on new technology to receive library services; a change in the availability of professionally educated librarians or other employees with specialized skills needed in libraries, just to name a few. Whenever there is a sustained movement (increasing or decreasing) in a direction of a demographic, behavioral, or psychographic factor, a trend can be said to be forming.

Futurists make predictions about trends that directly impact library operations. "There is increasing individualization in a growing global economy. Personal computers and cellular telephone technology, for example, move communication and information power to the level of the individual," wrote John Naisbitt and Patricia Aburdene in 1990.[2] Today this is common knowledge; nevertheless, many libraries are still struggling with how to adjust to these changes.

Trend watching is not a precision science. Librarians can become good trend watchers; they are keen observers. Additionally, business literature and the writings of futurists can be helpful in trend watching and trend extrapolation.

Trend Extrapolation

In its simplest form, trend extrapolation takes a single event or statistic and extends it into the future. Trend extrapolation can help librarians make projections about what is needed to serve particular segments of library users and potential users, now and in the future, but it should not be the only technique used to project needs. Following trends is like driving a car by watching the rearview mirror. You can see where you have been, but not where you are going. As John Guscott, editor and librarian at Lakewood Public Library, put it in an introduction to the Library Foresight System:[3]

> Library futurists use both qualitative and quantitative techniques in their speculation, including trend extrapolation, impact analyses, generational-consequences matrices, Delphi studies, scenario planning, relevance trees and simulations. These techniques do not foretell the future, but they turn up many types of futures, any of which we may try to make a reality.

The consideration of trends can be useful to all kinds of libraries with all sizes of budget; how useful depends on time, expertise, and other variables. The following is a partial list of sources for monitoring trends:

The Popcorn Report, Faith Popcorn (New York: Harper Business, 1992)

Library Futures Quarterly, Lakewood, OH: http://www.libraryfutures.com

LITA Top Tech Trends: http://www.lita.org/committee/toptech/

A Statistical Portrait of the United States: Social Conditions and Trends, 2d ed., Patricia C. Becker, ed. (Lanham, MD: Bernan, 2002)

Magazines: *American Demographics, Marketing News, Wired, Working Women, Esquire, Harper's, Prevention, Self, Architectural Digest*

Business journals: *Financial Times, Wall Street Journal, Fortune, Business Week, Forbes, US News and World Report*

Secondary data collected by planning commissions; corporate marketing audits

Why Consider Data Mining and Trend Analysis?

No doubt you have heard the term *data mining* associated with the expanded powers of the FBI under the USA PATRIOT Act. As a defender of the public's civil liberties, the thought of government officials sifting through data about what books are being read and what information is being sought from reference sources and on the Internet may offend your sensibilities. To avoid having to hand over data on library users, some librarians have resolved to limit the amount of data they keep on library users, updating their administrative procedures to call for the shredding of the day's transactions at the end of each day.

Well, if an army runs on its stomach, a business runs on data. You need data on the people in your community to help identify the needs of various segments of the community. You also need data about the library resources people in the community are currently using. Libraries and other organizations have access to mounds of data about the people in their communities. Zeroing in on just the data that will be useful in developing strategic plans and marketing plans is a positive use of data mining. Analyzing the trends in this data helps with your strategic and marketing planning, which includes your planning of promotional campaigns.

You can satisfy the business need for data and still protect the privacy of your library users. Simply strip the data of personally identifiable information—names, addresses, telephone numbers, and e-mail addresses. Just keep the demographic tags—gender, age, ethnic group, ZIP code, and the like.

WHAT ARE DEMOGRAPHICS?

Demographics are objective measures that describe the attributes of users in a community. Objective measures are those that can be observed or obtained from independent documentation, such as census reports. Decennial census data (and yearly updates) can be obtained from the U.S. Census Bureau website (http://www.census.gov), from reference books of government data, and from commercial software that facilitates easy manipulation and mapping of the census data. Powerful desktop mapping programs such as ArcView's Geographic Information System enable you to analyze statistical data and create custom-designed maps.

Geographic demographics are the objective measures that describe the attributes of your community. Measures such as an area population's size, density (rural, suburban, urban), and growth pattern (stable, negative, positive) have marketing implications for your products and services. Demographic statistics are useful in developing the marketing and public relations strategies and tactics referred to later in this book. Some of them are listed in figure 2-1.

FIGURE 2-1
Demographics

Public Libraries	Academic Libraries
Population density, e.g., rural, urban, suburban	Total enrollment (full-time, part-time, commuter, distance education, including distribution at locations other than main campus)
Population location (North, South, East, West)	Composition of the student body (number of freshmen, sophomores, juniors, seniors; master's, doctoral, postdoctoral students; members of international programs, honors programs)
Population size	
Population growth pattern, e.g., stable, negative, positive	
Gender	
Age, by ZIP code if possible	Off-campus locations of student body, by ZIP code
Family size	Degrees granted in various subject areas
Family life cycle, e.g., bachelorhood, newly married, full nest, empty nest	Types of degrees offered
	Total faculty size
Income, by ZIP code if possible	Percentages of faculty at various ranks (instructor, assistant, associate, or full professor)
Education	
Race and nationality (ethnic groups), as defined by the U.S. census categories	Faculty gender
	Faculty age
Occupation	Faculty ZIP codes
Number of public and private schools	Faculty academic department
Number of homeschooling families	Faculty research interests
Leading employers (industry types and number of employees)	Types of grants funded (e.g., medical research, sociological studies, development of entrepreneurial segments of the economy)
Media outlets: local, regional, national	

Many librarians in public libraries are already collecting data about their communities and library users as part of their long-range planning process. They have been using the planning models published by the Public Library Association. The most recent publication, *The New Planning for Results*, has an excellent tool for collecting community data.[4] Worksheets 2 and 3 are modified versions of this tool. Worksheet 2 may be used by public libraries and worksheet 3 by academic libraries to record data about their respective communities.

WHAT ARE BEHAVIORAL DATA?

Behavioral data are internal library statistics that describe the present and past behavior of library users. Some of these statistics can be culled from aggregate reports from a library's circulation system. Many marketers believe that behavioral variables are the best starting point for constructing market segments.[5] So, before you shred all that personally identifiable information, make sure you have captured the information in some aggregate report, a report that organizes all the data into groups that can be analyzed demographically. The most common behavioral variables used in marketing are *occasion of use*, *user status*, and *usage rate*.

Occasion of Use

Businesses have learned that buyers can be distinguished or grouped according to occasions when they purchase or use a product. For example, florists know that they are busy just before Mother's Day, on Valentine's Day, and during the graduation season. Certain types of flowers are preferred on these occasions, and the preferences may be associated with such demographic variables as gender, age, income level, or educational level of the buyer. Florists plan their promotional campaigns to coincide with these holidays, thus getting a bigger bang for their advertising buck.

Similarly, data on the occasions when library services are used should be gathered, including information on the services or resources used on specific occasions and demographic variables of the users. Some specific occasions to be observed and recorded are listed in figure 2-2.

User Status

You can establish the library user status of people in your communities. Then combine library user status and demographic variables with the type of services or resources used. Note you are not recording the titles and content being used by your library customers. For example, circulation staff and collection development staff may know that romance novels are heavily checked out by the young women in the community, who are regular library users. A program featuring romance authors may be a big success.

Knowledge of the types of services and resources used by library users of different status can provide a basis for strategies and tactics in the marketing plan. Categories of library user status might include the following:

> *Regular users.* Those who have used the library more than once a quarter in the past year.
>
> *Occasional users.* Those who have used the library more than once in the past year, but less than once a quarter.

FIGURE 2-2
Occasions to Use the Library

Public Libraries	Academic Libraries
Specific months when homework help is needed	One or two weeks before final exams
Specific months when students have reports due	Specific months when research papers are due
Holidays, when people seek information about traditional recipes, crafts, improving relationships, etc.	Specific months when thesis proposals or completed theses are due
Summer reading, young children, teens, and adults	Specific months that are deadlines for major research grant proposals
Announcement of movie releases of popular books for adults, teens, and young children	City/county, state, federal election-year cycles for candidate information
Months when people begin to engage in certain hobbies or recreational activities, e.g., gardening, boating, hunting	Spring career information searches, especially for seniors
Economic downturns, job hunting, career centers	Spring research on graduate schools
	Specific months when faculty research subjects for publications (scholarly journals and books), e.g., especially faculty on the tenure track
	Specific months when faculty research information to apply for grants

Infrequent users. Those who have used the library only once in the past year.

First-time users. Those who have just obtained a library card.

Former users. Those who have an expired library card.

These definitions and categories of user status are for purpose of illustration only. Each library may establish its own definitions and categories.

When you know the demographics of your library users, you can deduce who the non-users in the community are, as in the following example: A public library observes that its regular users are young mothers with preschool-age children, students enrolled in the nearby K–12 schools, and senior citizens. Its occasional users are women ages 30–40 in the upper-middle income bracket. You could deduce from these facts that non-users tend to be men ages 30–40 in any income bracket.

Usage Rate

Many markets can be grouped (segmented) into light-, medium-, and heavy-user groups. Marketers make a great effort to determine the demographic characteristics and media habits of the heavy users and aim their product offerings and promotional campaigns at them. This is preaching to the choir. All the same, getting your heavy users to take advantage of more of your services, especially your new offerings, creates loyal fans—and loyal fans can be counted on to speak up for the library during budget hearings or bond elections.

Traditionally, heavy users vary with different types of libraries. For example, the heavy users of public libraries are preschool children and their parents or other caregivers. Graduate students preparing dissertations are the heavy users of academic libraries. Special libraries such as corporate libraries cater to managers in strategic planning and marketing departments.

Use worksheets 2 or 3 to record data about the behavioral statistics of your library users.

LIBRARY RESOURCE DATA

Just as important as knowing about your existing and potential library users is knowing about the resources of your library—the staff, collection, equipment, technology, facility, and financial resources. An inventory of resources helps you determine if you have the capacity to meet the needs of your users today and in the future. *The New Planning for Results* has an excellent tool for collecting library resource data.

COLLECTING THE DATA

Collection of external demographic data and internal behavioral data is most often mentioned in relation to planning (strategic plans, long-range plans, planning for results, etc.). It is part of the *environmental scan* (also known as the community scan, community audit, or marketing audit) called for in models of most plans.

Collection of behavioral data from circulation systems is a sensitive issue because of the possibility of compromising the privacy of library users. You can alleviate the concerns about the privacy of users, however, by using the aggregate report capabilities of automated circulation systems.

Don't get bogged down collecting data. You may have already collected a lot of data in preparing your strategic plan. Use it. You don't have to collect everything suggested on the worksheets. Choose data that can be collected as quickly and easily as possible. Data for marketing is intended to provide a basis for segmenting users into groups; to uncover needs that can be satisfied with library services and resources; to identify the appropriate media to use to reach targeted segments; and to develop the appropriate message to appeal to the targeted segments.

If it is too difficult to collect precise or estimated numbers, you can classify your observations into qualitative categories such as "low," "medium," and "high" or "predominant," "increasing," and "decreasing." Just make sure there is a consensus among your library planners as to what these terms are meant to classify.

USING THE DATA

Once you have collected data, you must analyze it to look for trends. Pay special attention to areas that have increased or decreased from one period to another, perhaps using the ten-year federal census periods or five-year or annual planning cycles. Note the rate of change of data items. Has an item increased or decreased by 2 percent, 10 percent, or 50 percent? You may be able to compare trends observed in your data with state or national trends.

Spotting trends specific to certain geographic areas in the community can be facilitated by Geographic Information System (GIS) software. Although many GIS programs are designed to manipulate census or other government data sets, several allow use of an organization's own data (e.g., data from your circulation systems) to create custom maps. GIS programs are also helpful in developing plans to target specific geographic areas for promotional campaigns.

Studies by demographers, politicians, marketers, and social scientists have led to some relevant and instructive conclusions about the needs of library users based on their gender, ethnic origin, age, and other demographic variables. Age places people into generational cohorts: those born in 1945 or earlier are members of the Veteran, or Silent, generation; the baby boom generation are those born between 1946 and 1964; Generation Xers are those born between 1965 and 1985; and the Millennial generation are those born between 1986 and 2006. Members within a cohort have similar frames of reference in pop culture; baby boomers remember the hula hoop fad; Generation Xers remember bell-bottoms and platform shoes. Each of these generations perceives its need for library service differently. Being able to tap into each generation's frame of reference and relate it to your library's products and services increases the chances of successful promotional campaigns. Notice how businesses use songs from the 1960s to pitch products aimed at the baby boom generation.

As we have mentioned several times, collection and analysis of data about library users and non-users in the community helps uncover the needs and wants of specific groups of people (market segments) whom the library may decide to target for several of its service offerings. But just collecting and analyzing demographic or behavioral data does not give in-depth insight into key topics such as these:

- who uses or does not use the library's services
- why services are used or not used
- how the library might change what it offers to motivate use of its services
- what new services are needed
- which services could be discontinued

In the past twenty to thirty years, businesses have answered these types of questions about their customers by using demographic data in conjunction with psychographics (social, psychological, and consumer decision-making analysis data). Some libraries have also begun to use psychographics and information from generational cohort literature to program services for their users.

What Is Psychographics?

Psychographics is a technique with which lifestyles are measured.[6] Lifestyles are manifested in people's activities, interests, and opinions (AIOs), which can be measured by long questionnaires (25–90 pages). Figure 2-3 shows the major dimensions used to measure AIO elements.

In the AIO questionnaires, people are asked to agree or disagree with statements such as these: "I would like to become an actor." "I enjoy going to concerts." "I usually dress for fashion, not for comfort." "I often have a cocktail before dinner." The responses are then fed into computers and sorted into lifestyle categories. Names are given to certain lifestyles, such as Hippies, Yuppies, Traditionalists. A formal classification of lifestyles has emerged from geo-demographic analysis (the study of demographic variables combined with AIOs of a specific neighborhood). Several companies have developed classifications schemes for commercial use.

One company, Claritas, regarded as the leading provider of intelligent marketing information and marketing services, pioneered geodemography under the PRIZM (Potential Rating Index by ZIP Markets) name in the mid-1970s. PRIZM was based on the sociological premise that "birds of a feather flock together," that people with similar demographic traits tend to behave in the same way in the marketplace.

FIGURE 2.3
The AIO Framework

Activities	Interests	Opinions
Work	Family	Themselves
Hobbies	Home	Social Issues
Social Events	Job	Politics
Vacation	Community	Business
Entertainment	Recreation	Economics
Club Membership	Fashion	Education
Community	Food	Products
Shopping	Media	Future
Sports	Achievements	Culture

Source: Joseph T. Plummer, "The Concept and Application of Life-Style Segmentation,"
Journal of Marketing 38 (January 1974): 34.

In 2003 the company introduced PRIZM New Evolution, a revolutionary segmentation system that, for the first time, harnessed the power of both household- and geographic-level data. "With PRIZM NE, Claritas has created a seamless transition between household-level segmentation and traditional geodemographics by providing the same segments at both levels," said Claritas president Robert Nascenzi. "Having the ability to 'downshift' from geodemographics to household-level targeting makes it possible for marketers to move seamlessly from market planning and media strategy, to customer acquisition, cross-selling and retention."[7]

According to a press release introducing PRIZM NE, the new system has grown from sixty-two to sixty-six segments to reflect America's increasing diversity over the past decade. Here are some of the more notable new segments:[8]

Young Digerati, No. 4. With the boom in new computer and digital technology, this cluster represents the nation's tech-savvy singles and couples living in fashionable neighborhoods on the urban fringe.

Beltway Boomers, No. 17. The nation's baby boomers are now in their forties and fifties, and this segment reflects one group of college-educated, upper-middle-class homeowners. Like many of their peers who married late and are still raising children, these boomers live in comfortable suburban subdivisions and are still pursuing child-centered lifestyles.

Fast-Track Families, No. 20. The migration of upscale city dwellers out to the countryside can be seen in the emergence of this ex-urban cluster. The Fast-Track Families segment is filled with middle-aged parents who have the disposable income and educated sensibility for a granola-and-grits lifestyle: they fish, boat, and shop over the Internet—all at high rates.

The Cosmopolitans, No. 26. The continued gentrification of the nation's cities has resulted in the emergence of this segment—concentrated in America's fast-growing metros such as Las Vegas, Miami, and Albuquerque. These households feature older homeowners, empty nesters, and college graduates who enjoy leisure-intensive lifestyles.

Multi-Culti Mosaic, No. 54. Capturing some of the growth of new immigrants to the United States—Hispanics now number 38 million people—this cluster is the urban home for a mixed populace of younger Hispanic, Asian, and African American singles and families. With nearly a quarter of the residents foreign-born, the Multi-Culti Mosaic segment is a mecca for first-generation Americans who are striving to improve their lower-middle-class status.

Old Milltowns, No. 57. With the shrinking of the nation's manufacturing sector, America's once-thriving factory towns have aged, as have their residents. Old Milltowns reflect the decline of these small industrial communities, now filled with retired singles and couples living quietly on fixed incomes. These home-centered residents make up one of the top segments for daytime television.

PRIZM NE also reflects that part of the American landscape that has not completely changed over the past decade. Lifestyle segments still featured in PRIZM NE include *Upper Crust*, *Pools & Patios*, *Movers & Shakers*, *Bohemian Mix*, *Shotguns and Pickups*, *Golden Ponds*, and *Kids & Cul-de-Sacs*.

The sixty-six segments in PRIZM NE are grouped into fourteen broader social groups indicated by the degree of urbanization, from rural countryside to urban high-rises. At the top of both the affluence scale and density scale is Social Group U1, Urban Uptown, which includes *Young Digerati*, *Money & Brains*, *Bohemian Mix*, *The Cosmopolitans*, and *American Dreams*. At the opposite extreme—with relatively low affluence and low-density housing—is Social Group T4, Rustic Living, which comprises *Young & Rustic*, *Golden Ponds*, *Crossroads Villagers*, *Old Milltowns*, *Back Country Folks*, and *Bedrock America*.[9] Figure 2-4 illustrates the demographic data provided about a few of the segments.

For a fee, Claritas provides a customized report listing all the ZIP codes in a selected area with lifestyle information. Libraries may find these a valuable tool. The report could suggest good targets for fund-raising or target segments for services and resources. To give companies a flavor for some of the lifestyles in different communities, Claritas has provided a free program on the Web called "You Are Where You Live" (YAWYL) (http://www.yawyl.claritas .com). YAWYL allows access to a limited amount of demographic data from the census combined with lifestyle traits, such as preferences for entertainment, eating establishments, media outlets, types of cars, and hobbies. When a ZIP code is entered into the online program, a profile of the five most common PRIZM NE lifestyle segments in the community is generated.

John Guscott at the Lakewood Public Library used YAWYL and a customized report to learn more about the residents in his library's service area. This library also used *The Clustering of America*, written by Michael J. Weiss, to expand its collection and develop programs to attract a segment of non-users to the library. In 2000 Weiss wrote a second book about the consumer segments of the United States and several other countries, *The Clustered World*, which may help librarians better understand their customers.[10] "PRIZM NE could be an excellent tool for librarians to use to develop a marketing campaign," says Weiss:[11]

> First, librarians may need to familiarize themselves with lifestyle segmentation by reading books on the subject or going on the Web [You Are Where You Live (YAWYL)] to use the ZIP code look-up program to find out about lifestyles of the people in their serving area. Also, librarians should find out about the demographics of their patrons, determining their income and education level, to better understand their patrons' backgrounds. Combine this information with an understanding of their patrons' lifestyle activities, such as the issues people care about, their hobbies, what they do on a Saturday night, or where they go on a Sunday morning. Use this knowledge to stock the library's shelves with books and materials to reflect the lifestyles of their patrons. Set up window displays to reflect the lifestyle themes of the patrons in the serving area. Let your customers know what your library has to offer.

FIGURE 2-4
Selected PRIZM NE Segments: An Illustration of Information Provided

Social Group	Cluster	Nickname	Age Range	Key Education Level(s)	Employment	W	B	A	H
U1	04	Young Digerati	<45	College graduates+	Executive, Professional, White-Collar	✓		✓	✓
S2	17	Beltway Boomers	35–64	College	Professional, White-Collar	✓		✓	
T1	20	Fast-Track Families	25–54	College	White-Collar	✓			
U1	26	The Cosmopolitans	55+	Some college	White-Collar	✓	✓	✓	✓
U2	54	Multi-Culti Mosaic	25–54	Elem. school High school	White-Collar, Service, Blue-Collar		✓	✓	✓
T4	57	Old Milltowns	55+	Elem. school High school	White-Collar, Service, Blue-Collar	✓	✓		

Source: Adapted from Claritas PRIZM NE Social Groups Poster, copyright 2004, Claritas, Inc. "PRIZM" and "Claritas" are registered trademarks of Claritas, Inc. The sixty-six PRIZM segment nicknames ("Blue Blood Estates," "Big Sky Families," "Country Squires," etc.) are trademarks of Claritas, Inc. All rights reserved.

Note: W=White, B=Black, A=Asian, H=Hispanic

Secondary Sources of Demographic and Psychographic Data

Advertising Age magazine: http://adage.com

Bernan Essential Government Information: http://www.bernan.com

Black Enterprise magazine, E. G. Graves Publishing, New York: http://www
.blackenterprise.com

*Editor and Publisher Market Guide 2005: The Directory of Newspaper Markets and
Demographics*, 81st ed. (Denville, NJ: VNU Business Publications, 2004):
http://www.editorandpublisher.com

Commercial Atlas and Market Guide (Rand McNally) includes detailed maps, census
data and population estimates, economic data, economic activity projections, and
more: http://www.randmcnally.com

Annual Survey of Buying Power issue of *Sales and Marketing Management* magazine
(VNU Business Publications): http://www.salesandmarketing.com

Futurist magazine, World Future Society, Bethesda, MD: http://www.wfs.org/
futurist.htm

U.S. Census (http://www.census.gov) provides many data sources, such as American
FactFinder (http://factfinder.census.gov); census release date list (http://www
.census.gov/population/www/censusdata/c2kproducts.html); economic census;
population and household data; state data centers; Statistical Abstract of the
United States; and Supplemental Survey (http://www.census.gov/c2ss/www/
index.html)

Why We Buy, Paco Underhill (New York: Simon and Schuster, 2000)

Wired magazine, St. Martin's Press, New York

Local newspapers

School enrollment

DRAWING CONCLUSIONS FROM THE DATA

During the course of gathering and reviewing data on your entire universe of users, you may
come to some conclusions about the needs and wants of groups of users or non-users. You
may determine (1) that existing products or services satisfy a specific target market; (2) that
modifications are needed to existing products or services to satisfy the target market; or (3)
that a new product or service should be developed to satisfy that market. See chapter 4 for a
discussion of product and service offerings. See chapter 5 for more information on selecting
a target market.

1. In lieu of gathering a lot of formal statistics from the census and city/county planning departments, library staff and board members can institute an annual observation period.

2. Observe what is happening in the library branch(es) and in the community.

3. Ask questions:

   What is going on in my community? What is different from one year ago? five years ago?

   What is going on in the library profession, in terms of management practices? in terms of technology?

   How will these changes impact my library? What impact do these changes have on the types of services my library can offer?

4. Record your observations and assumptions about the impact of changes.

5. Supplement your observations with government data, if easily available.

6. Make discussions of observations and assumptions a regular part of staff meetings, at least once a year.

7. Make discussions of observations and assumptions a regular part of library board meetings, at least once a year.

NOTES

1. Evan St. Lifer, "Tapping into the Zen of Marketing," *Library Journal* (May 2001): 44–45. In 2003 a new segmentation system, PRIZM NE, was introduced. In the PRIZM NE system, the segment nicknamed "Urban Achievers" has been updated and may have somewhat different characteristics than the Urban Achievers cluster described in the 1999 PRIZM system.

2. John Naisbitt and Patricia Aburdene, *Megatrends 2000: Ten New Directions for the 1990's* (New York: William Morrow, 1990), 302.

3. J. Guscott, "Introduction to the Library Foresight System, *Library Futures Quarterly* (2002), http://www.libraryfutures.com/lfs.htm.

4. Sandra Nelson, for the Public Library Association, *The New Planning for Results* (Chicago: American Library Association, 2001), 282–286, 291–295.

5. P. Kotler, *Marketing Management: Analysis, Planning and Control* (Englewood Cliffs, NJ: Prentice-Hall, 1984).

6. For more on psychographics, see J. R. Evans and B. Berman, *Marketing* (New York: Macmillan, 1985); J. F. Engel and R. D. Blackwell, *Consumer Behavior* (Hinsdale, IL: Dryden Press, 1982); P. Kotler, *Kotler on Marketing: How to Create, Win and Dominate Markets* (New York: Free Press, 1999); and Kotler, *Marketing Management: Analysis, Planning and Control* (Englewood Cliffs, NJ: Prentice-Hall, 1984).

7. Robert Nascenzi, "Claritas Introduces Revolutionary New PRIZM Segmentation System," Claritas press release, San Diego, CA, 2003.

8. Segment definitions drawn from Stephen F. Moore, "Claritas Introduces Revolutionary New PRIZM Segmentation System," Claritas press release, San Diego, CA, 2003.

9. Groupings drawn from Claritas, Inc., "Claritas PRIZM NE, Social Groups," Claritas poster, San Diego, CA, 2004.

10. Michael J. Weiss, *The Clustering of America* (New York: HarperCollins, 1988), describes the forty neighborhood PRIZM clusters that existed in the fifty states in the late 1980s. Weiss, *The Clustered World* (Boston: Little, Brown, 2000), reexamines the nation, finding that it has fragmented into sixty-two PRIZM clusters; Weiss also examines the cluster concept in other nations.

11. Weiss, telephone interview, February 22, 2005.

three

Developing the Marketing Plan

Getting Started

Plans are nothing; planning is everything.

—Dwight D. Eisenhower

---

1. Define *marketing* as a process that includes more than promotional activity.
2. Show the "military" roots of marketing planning.
3. Introduce the structure of the marketing plan.

When Linda Marie Golian-Lui told her reference librarians that she wanted them to wear army boots and fatigues, they were sure she had lost it. This University of Florida library director asked her staff to be a little daring when they gave BLT (Basic Library Training) to freshmen and other new students. They used a military theme in their PowerPoint presentation and in the handouts and advertisements they created. The librarians wore their "uniforms" when they gave classes. Their T-shirts sported a library logo. They caused a stir; neither they nor their campus has been the same since.[1]

Some data gathering, analysis, and planning preceded Director Golian-Lui's instructions to her reference librarians. The University of Florida library's strategic plan identified freshmen and other new students as target markets on which to focus. A goal of "being daring" was set, and one of the strategic directives was to develop a marketing plan to promote the library to these target markets.

One of the goals of this book is to encourage librarians to embrace the concept that marketing is more than promotion. Marketing is the process of facilitating an exchange of something of value for something needed. Marketing is about understanding the needs of your customers and providing a product or service to fill those needs at a place and at a price they are willing to pay to complete the exchange.

Product, Place, Price, and Promotion are components of the *marketing mix*. Promotion is the last step in the marketing process. Another goal of this book is to demystify these con-

24

cepts. We use hypothetical scenarios for a generic service—chat reference—to illustrate marketing concepts. In this particular illustration, teenagers are the target market, but the principles discussed are applicable to any target market.

PLANNING ORIGINS

The business approach to developing strategic and marketing plans comes from the military. The hierarchy of plans, sections within plans, strategy, and tactics all relate to war planning. The business world really does consider the fight to obtain customers—willing to exchange something of value for the product or service being offered—as going to war with competitors. Although this thought may not be easy to accept, libraries are indeed in competition, not only with bookstores but with other departments on campus or other public departments providing services to the community.

Fighting for customers may go against the grain for the typical librarian, who is more likely to be saying, "I don't have to fight for customers; I have more customers than I can handle with my limited staff and materials resources." But the truth is that libraries must fight for a share of the tax dollar or academic institution's budget. To be effective, a library must show its elected officials and administrators that its services are in demand by the taxpayers, students, faculty, and other customer groups—that these constituents are willing to exchange their valuable time for the library's products and services and are delighted with the library experience their tax dollar or tuition is providing. Moreover, the services your library provides have value to the larger community as well as the user. The best way to show value is to have a plan that analyzes the target market for a specific service, has strategies and tactics to encourage use of the service, and has methods to monitor the effectiveness of those strategies and tactics.

TYPES OF MARKETING PLANS

In the business world, a separate marketing plan is developed for each new product and is updated annually—as a separate marketing plan or as part of a product/service family marketing plan—until the product is discontinued.

Existing Product/Service Marketing Plans

In most cases, library marketing plans are developed for an existing product, service, or product/service family. Reference services are considered a product/service family, encompassing such individual services as in-house reference desk service, telephone reference, business reference, one-on-one reference by appointment, e-mail reference, and chat reference.

Existing product/service marketing plans are also referred to as annual marketing plans, because it is assumed that the plan developed for the new product has been updated annually—to reflect changes in the target market and competition; to set new goals and objectives for the upcoming year; and to develop new strategies and tactics for the marketing mix (product, place, price, and promotion).

In most cases, you will be developing an existing product/service marketing plan from scratch. However, because the product or service has been in use, data on how your customers use it and on the competitive alternatives should be readily available. Gaps in data can always be filled in with educated guesses or assumptions. Just remember to document all your assumptions carefully so that they can be confirmed, amended, or discarded as you monitor the plan.

New Product/Service Marketing Plans

The new product/service plan is developed with sketchy information because there is no history on how the target market will use the product/service or on how your library provides the product/service. Marketing professor William A. Cohen advises:[2]

> With a new product/service plan, it is sometimes necessary to make assumptions based on similar products or services that the company has marketed or that have been introduced by other companies. But remember: if you use information based on other companies' experiences, you must assess your ability to duplicate their performance. Other sources of information may be necessary to modify data from other companies' experiences.

Librarians often model their new service introductions after services that have been introduced by other libraries. For example, the idea of having an entire community read one book and discuss it was not new when the Flint Public Library in Michigan set out to encourage a sense of community through the shared experience of reading a book to stimulate a discussion of community issues. The librarians and community partners on the planning committee were deliberate in their efforts to customize the event for their community.

Activities surrounding the first community read, *The Watsons Go to Birmingham* by Flint native Christopher Paul Curtis, included a visit by the author to talk with hundreds of children and to see a dramatic adaptation of his book. There were also public readings, discussion groups, and online chats. Selecting the book for their third year, James McBride's *The Color of Water*, involved soliciting recommendations from the community at large and hosting a book buffet at which the top fifteen books suggested were presented in animated book talks. Participants then cast their votes by placing dots on large replicas of each book's cover. The introduction of the One Book–One Community program was a resounding success, demonstrated by the library's winning the 2004 National Library Service Award for extraordinary public service.[3]

Librarians in Flint modified the experience of other libraries to fit their community by constructing ways to get community involvement in the planning. Another method of modifying data is to test assumptions in focus groups or in a product/service trial. Such trials are limited in scope (geography, customers, resources, or time).

The steering committee in charge of developing a promotional campaign for emergent literacy services in Maryland public libraries avoided a close call by testing their campaign logo in focus groups located throughout the state. One focus group called the child in the logo "ghost boy." Lillie Dyson, then chief of the Division of Library Services at the state library of Maryland, was mortified when she heard this: "The campaign materials need to appeal to parents of young children, not repel them." The steering committee quickly came up with another logo—a charming baby girl, who subsequently made a big hit. What a close call that was.[4]

THE STRUCTURE OF THE MARKETING PLAN

Just like an outline of a position paper or the table of contents of a book, marketing plans have several sections, which vary in detail depending on the preferences of decision makers and the purpose of the plan. Typical plan purposes include providing a "road map" to state how to reach goals and objectives in a logical way; securing funding for promotional campaigns to increase awareness and usage of a service; and justifying a decision to continue providing a service or introducing a new one.

Although the format of marketing plan outlines may differ, most marketing plans have the following sections: table of contents, executive summary, product/service description, target market description, assessment of the current marketing situation, opportunity and issue analysis, marketing goals and objectives, marketing strategies, marketing tactics, implementation and controls, summary, and appendices. Figure 3-1 lists these sections and their purposes. For-profit business marketing plans also include a section to examine the expected financial payoff in the form of a projected profit/loss statement. You may want to include a financial section in your marketing plan to show the costs of providing an existing or new service. Increasingly, librarians are asked to show that the cost of a service is worth the benefits it provides.

If your marketing plan is to be used as an internal road map to reach your goals and objectives, you may make it only a few pages long, with each section being explained in a paragraph or two. Or you could use worksheet 4, the Marketing Plan Template; fill in the sections and house it in a three-ring binder, without narrative explanations. If the marketing plan is to be used to secure resources or if it will receive external review, you may want to devote a couple of pages of narrative text to each section. If the marketing plan accomplishes its purpose and helps you achieve your goals and objectives, whatever form you choose is fine. The process of developing the plan will be of tremendous benefit to you.

In the following chapters we discuss each section of a marketing plan in detail. In several chapters, an illustration of a completed section of worksheet 4 is provided based on the example of chat reference—a service in the reference services family of products offered by public and academic libraries.

FIGURE 3-1
Contents of a Marketing Plan

Section	Purpose
Table of Contents	Allows several members of a review board to get to their section of interest quickly.
Executive Summary	Synopsis of the entire plan for quick management skimming.
I. Introduction	Presents an explanation of the details of the product/service. After reading it, the evaluator should understand what the product/service is and what the library proposes to do with it.
II. Target Market Description	Describes the target market in detail by using demographics, psychographics, and behavioral data with respect to your product/service, geography, and lifestyle. Indicates how large the target market is and why it was selected for the product/service.
III. Current Market Situation	Analyzes where and how the product/service is currently being obtained (place); the price being paid (negative barriers to use or fees); the competitive alternatives; the product/service's current position in the customer's mind; and relevant background information on the macroenvironment.
IV. Opportunity and Issue Analysis	Summarizes the main opportunities and threats for the product/service, the strengths and weaknesses of the library, and issues facing the product/service that the plan must deal with.
V. Marketing Goals and Objectives	States precisely the goals and objectives in terms of measurable changes in variables such as awareness, usage, and funding, along with the time needed to achieve them.
VI. Marketing Strategies	Presents the broad marketing approach to be used to meet the plan's goals and objectives and how budget decisions will be made to support the strategies.
VII. Marketing Tactics / Action Plan	Answers what will be done, who will do it, when will it be done, and how much it will cost in terms of the product, price, place, partnerships, and promotion.
VIII. Implementation and Controls	Outlines the controls to be applied to monitor the plan's progress, facilitating the monitoring of tactics to determine if they are being implemented on schedule and according to budget.
IX. Summary	Summarizes the advantages the product/service has over the competitive alternatives and why the plan will succeed.
X. Appendixes	Include all supporting information.

Source: Adapted from W. A. Cohen, *The Marketing Plan,* 2d ed. (New York: John Wiley, 1998); and P. Kotler, *Marketing Management: Analysis, Planning and Control* (Englewood Cliffs, NJ: Prentice-Hall, 1984).

NOTES

1. Linda Golian-Lui, telephone interview, April 29, 2003.
2. W. A. Cohen, *The Marketing Plan*, 2d ed. (New York: John Wiley, 1998), 5.
3. Flint Public Library, "Flint Public Library's National Award for Public Library Service," http://www.flint.lib.mi.us, 2004.
4. Lillie Dyson, telephone interview, July 3, 2003.

four

Marketing Plan Introduction
Product/Service Details

> *The single most important element of the organization's marketing mix is its offer. . . . Most organizations, for-profit and nonprofit, cannot survive for very long if they do not offer something fundamentally attractive. Further, they cannot grow if they cannot distinguish their offer in significant ways from the competition, even when the "competition" is inaction or the status quo. Even the most creative and dramatic advertising cannot "sell" a fundamentally weak offering.*
>
> —Philip Kotler and Alan R. Andreasen,
> *Strategic Marketing for NonProfit Organizations*

chapter objectives

1. Provide information needed to write the introduction to the marketing plan; this includes a product/service description.

2. Explain the elements that make up a product/service offer.

3. Discuss how products or services you offer are related in families and in an overall hierarchy.

4. Introduce the concept of the product life cycle applied to library products and services.

5. Discuss partnerships and collaborative efforts as a way to supplement resources needed to deliver products and services.

When the University of Washington library developed its service description for a new reference service—chat reference—they decided on the following description: "Q&A Live is an exciting, new reference service of the University of Washington. This service allows anyone with an Internet connection to chat in real-time with reference librarians who are able to answer questions and help find resources. 'Virtual' reference services either provide the specific answers you need or direct you to the appropriate online and hardcopy resources. With Q&A Live, users who are in need of reference materials can find what they are looking for faster and easier."[1]

The product/service description for Q&A Live is a good example of an effective service description. It states what the service is, for whom the service is intended, and what benefit the service offers the user. This is the kind of description that should be contained in the introduction of a marketing plan.

In this example, the University of Washington library is promoting a single library service to an identified target market or multiple markets. At the same time, students and faculty who use this service will also become acquainted with other services offered by the library. And, more important, they will interact with the librarians and the library's resources. They will come to recognize the expertise of the librarians and the value they provide. It is far better to develop individual marketing plans with service descriptions for your services than to describe what you have to offer as a large collection of materials available for borrowing, along with a few computers available for public use and a staff that can assist with questions. The introduction for each marketing plan should describe the service in detail and how it fits into the market. In this chapter we discuss how this is accomplished.

A marketing plan begins with the most important element of the marketing mix—the product or service you intend to offer. According to marketing professor William A. Cohen,

> the introduction of the marketing plan is the explanation of the details of your project. Unlike the executive summary, it is not an overview of the project. Its purpose is to give the background of the project and to describe your product or service so that any reader will understand exactly what you are proposing. The introduction can be a fairly large section. After reading it, the reader should understand what the product or service is and what you propose to do with it.[2]

Worksheet 4, the Marketing Plan Template, is a tool for developing your marketing plan. In it, section I, Introduction, presents a series of questions geared to help you explain the details of your product or service and how it fits into the market. The information needed to answer these questions is discussed in this chapter. In addition, figure 4-3, at the end of this chapter, is an example of a completed introduction for a chat reference service.

WHAT ARE THE BENEFITS OF THE PRODUCT/SERVICE OFFER?

Core Benefits

What products and services have in common is that customers acquire both for what they can do for them, that is, for the positive consequences they deliver—the core benefits. For example, some customers are entertained by a good mystery. When the librarian recommends a mystery and walks a customer to the shelf to obtain it while telling her a little about the book, the customer is experiencing excellent customer service and enjoying a preview of the core benefit to come—entertainment. Another customer's need for convenient and quick access to information to answer a question is satisfied when a reference librarian leads him to a source that will answer the question—whether he is sitting at a computer or via the telephone. The customer gets his answer quickly—the core benefit. He has acquired a reliable source of information and he can take advantage of his knowledge.

Organizations that are customer-centered rather than organization-centered strive to develop their products and services to anticipate and meet the needs and wants of the customer. In fact, customer-centered organizations strive to have products and services that surprise and delight their customers. According to Ken Blanchard and Sheldon Bowles, "Three secrets to turning your customers into raving fans are: 1) decide what your vision is of your product/service; 2) discover what your customers want . . . make adjustments to bring your vision in line with what customers want; and 3) consistently deliver the vision plus one percent. . . . Consistency is the key to delivering Raving Fan Service."[3]

Social Benefits

In addition to delivering positive consequences (core benefits) to the customer, library products and services can also provide positive consequences (social benefits) to the community or campus. Young children who are read to, for example, are being entertained, but they also do better in school; thus school test scores are higher; community schools with high test scores attract more residents, which increases the tax base; increases in the tax base pay for more services for everyone in the community. Similarly, college students who make use of library services are more successful in their classes, and more of them graduate; high graduation rates enhance the reputation of the college; successful graduates make contributions to society at all levels; distinguished alumni further enhance the reputation of the college, and appreciative alumni make monetary gifts to their alma mater.

The practice of developing marketing plans to entice a target market to use or increase usage of a product or service that has social benefits is called *social marketing*. Dissuading a target market from using a product or service in a way that would be harmful to the community is another aspect of social marketing.

WHAT ARE THE CHARACTERISTICS OF THE PRODUCT/SERVICE OFFER?

Both products and services have characteristics. The marketing plan's introduction is the place to discuss how you will manage the various aspects of the offering's characteristics. In the majority of cases libraries will be offering services, so from this point on we refer to library offerings as *services*. In this chapter we address both products and services, but we devote more attention to the characteristics and management of services.

Product Characteristics

A product is a tangible item with some or all of these five characteristics:

Features. A book has pages bound by a front and back cover.

Styling. Books come in various genres with varying size, shape, and number of pages.

Quality level. A book is written well or badly.

Packaging. Books come with various front covers or dust jackets designed to make the book appealing and quickly convey its type of content.

Brand name. The "For Dummies" book series is an example of a brand name.

Service Characteristics

Philip Kotler and Alan Andreasen define a *service* as "any activity or benefit that one party can offer to another that is essentially intangible and does not result in the ownership of anything. Its production may or may not be tied to a physical product." Intangibility and other service characteristics are discussed by Kotler and Andreasen in *Strategic Marketing for NonProfit Organizations*, on which this section is based.[4]

1. Services are *intangible*. That is, they cannot be seen, tasted, felt, heard, or smelled before they are bought. When a librarian answers a reference question for a customer, he or she is providing a service that uses the library's collection, databases, or Internet resources, but it is not tied to a physical product the customer will "possess," even briefly. The customer cannot know the content or value of the service in advance, since there is no tangible product involved. Customers use the service on the basis of secondary cues and their confidence in the service provider.

You can make the service appear tangible by providing secondary cues and giving customers a reason to have confidence in the quality of your staff and resources. Diplomas and evidence of certification signify the quality of a physician or a mechanic; plaques and awards are signs that a restaurant or museum is noteworthy; libraries can display plaques and awards in lobbies and at reference desks and mention them in newsletters and on websites. Give your services brand names to make each service more memorable. "Atmospherics" such as the way staff is dressed, the quality of the brochures used to describe the offerings, or the character of the external architecture and interiors of the building can affect customer expectations. You can also provide tangible mementos of the service. For example, restaurants provide after-dinner mints. Libraries can provide transcripts of chat reference sessions.

2. **Services are *inseparable* from the source that provides them.** Customers interact with library staff to obtain services. In many cases, librarians use low-tech or high-tech aids to provide the service offering. The librarian conducting story hour may use "big books," cutouts and a flannel board, or puppets to read expressively to children. Librarians who provide a reader's advisory service may rely on paper lists (or bookmarks) prepared by the collection development librarian (e.g., Tom Clancy–type adventure novels; Civil War romance novels), or they may use a computerized system that generates a list of novels based on a title or author the customer has enjoyed reading. Librarians who staff the virtual reference desk to provide chat reference use instant messaging software to chat in real-time interactive sessions with customers.

Since the services are so often indistinguishable from the person delivering them, you must encourage all staff—professional and support staff—to become "customer-obsessed" and technology savvy. You want to build relationships with your customers. You cannot afford to have surly, unpleasant, technologically challenged staff mar the service experience for your customers.

3. **Services can be highly *variable* depending on who is providing them and when they are provided.** Legal advice from a high court justice is likely to be of higher quality than advice from a recently graduated attorney.

You can maximize the quality and consistency of your service offerings: develop good personnel selection and training programs; establish routine procedures, policies, and forms for the service in all branches; develop adequate customer satisfaction monitoring systems.

4. **Services are *perishable*.** They cannot be stored. A car can be kept in inventory until it is sold, but a librarian giving bibliographic instruction to ten people when thirty were expected is likely a waste of resources.

Librarians managing services must try to bring supply and demand into balance. On the demand side, you can institute a service reservations system that allows you to cancel an offering if there is not enough interest. Or you can develop promotional campaigns to increase use of the offering in nonpeak time periods. On the supply side, you can use part-time staff to provide offerings during peak demand; you can develop ways to have customers participate in service delivery such as self–check out during busy times; you can develop partnerships with other libraries, businesses, and other entities to complement or supplement your capabilities to meet the demand for services—for example, chat reference or rewards for summer reading.

5. **Many service exchanges *involve the customer* as an integral part of the production of the service itself.** The customer therefore plays a crucial role in the ultimate nature and quality of the experience. What does the customer have to know to use your service? Will the customer need to know how to manipulate a mouse in order to use the library's online catalog? Must a customer understand how to follow prompts on a computer screen menu to obtain

a recommended list of novels to read? Do students know that faculty put materials on reserve for their information? Are there special ways of retrieving reserve materials? Must your customer know how to phrase a reference question properly in order to get a useful source of information from the chat reference service? Does she know that the reference librarian is not doing the work for her but is providing reliable sources of information on the topic? If the customer does not possess the skills needed to use the service, how will she obtain them?

Customers who know how to consume your service will have a "delightful" experience. Delighted customers will become raving fans. You must teach them what they need to know to consume your service, or you must change your service to fit what they know. You must also manage their expectations. "A major source of dissatisfaction on the part of many service customers is not inferior service but exaggerated expectations," write Kotler and Andreasen.

The characteristics of your service should be identified in the marketing plan's introduction. Remember that the people reading the plan to determine if it gets approved may not understand library jargon or technical terms related to a service; you must be able to tell these readers how your service functions in simple, nontechnical terms. If you think your service needs changing or the customer needs education to use it, you must address this in developing your goals, objectives, and strategies.

WHAT RESOURCES DO YOU NEED TO DELIVER THE SERVICE?

Library Resources

Do you have the right materials in the collection to provide a service? Do you have enough staff hours and staff with the right kinds of skill? Do you have the right kind of equipment and infrastructure? Should you reallocate resources from services that are meeting the needs of a small number of users to the service for which you have chosen to develop a marketing plan? Let your strategic plan be your guide about seeking additional resources. If offering the service is consistent with one or more of the strategic directives, you are on solid ground by developing goals, objectives, strategies, and tactics to increase resources for the service. Your marketing plan can be an invaluable tool to help persuade your funding bodies to provide additional resources, to obtain a grant to provide the service, or to solicit partners to supplement your resources.

Partnerships

Librarians at all levels in all kinds of libraries are increasingly expected to either form or participate in partnerships, collaborations, or consortiums. This is new territory for most. In today's economic climate of decreased funding and expectations of getting more "bang for the buck," collaboration is essential. The energy and ideas generated through collaboration can be well worth the effort and bring forth creative solutions to problems. But there can also be competition, abrasion, criticism, one-upmanship, and other divisive attitudes and behaviors. Often what starts off positively enough ends up feeling like two porcupines hugging. In a collaborative effort, we are looking for results that could not be achieved alone.

Four librarians in Baltimore, Maryland, had a spark of genius while meeting for their customary Friday coffee. Wouldn't it be exciting to be able to share each other's collections and provide library users, students, and artists with online access? Thus began a collaboration among eight institutions: the Maryland Historical Society; Johns Hopkins University; Baltimore Museum of Art; Maryland Institute College of Art; University of Maryland, Baltimore County; Walters Art Museum; Enoch Pratt Free Library; and Maryland State Department of Education. The collaborative effort is known as the Baltimore Arts Resource Online Consortium (BAROC). With federal and local funding, members of BAROC worked with a Baltimore-based technology vendor, the Berndt Group, to develop Maryland ArtSource, which features six categories of access for the material: "Artists," "Institutions," "Art Collections Online," "Library Catalogs," "What's New," and "Maryland ArtMail." "The shared commitment among the BAROC partner institutions to promoting widespread awareness of the important and diverse art holdings and library collections that our institutions represent has made Maryland ArtSource possible. By joining together, we have pooled our institutional expertise into a single resource and simultaneously advanced the educational missions of our respective institutions," said Tom Beck, chairman of BAROC and chief curator of the Albin O. Kuhn Library and Gallery of the University of Maryland, Baltimore County.[5]

You can view the end result of this collaboration at http://www.marylandartsource.org. The introduction to the marketing plan for this service would include some mention of the partners and the steps planned to make their collaboration successful.

Experts on collaboration recommend these steps:[6]

1. **Clearly define the mission, vision, goals, and objectives of the collaborative effort.** This is not easy to do. Even when these are defined, the words may have differing meanings to the individuals involved. One way to counter this problem is to "start with the end in mind"—in other words, to answer the question, What will it look like when we get there? Ultimately, the collaborating group needs a shared vision.

2. **Bring every potential stakeholder to the table in the beginning.** This is especially important for a fairly short-term collaboration. For long-term collaborative efforts, having tiers of participants might be more effective. Who comes to the table can make or break the effort, so choose carefully and strategically. Be very clear about the potential risks and benefits of including a group or individual.

3. **Establish ground rules at the first meeting and keep them visible during each meeting.** Six or eight, no more than ten, ground rules is a good number. If someone does not offer a ground rule, specifically ask that person for input. Ground rules are important. Some common rules are to start and end on time, to treat differences as information, and to go for consensus.

4. **Always provide an agenda of announcements, accomplishments, issues, and actions.** This will help provide a framework and production-oriented approach for each meeting. With this kind of process, people's time and input are more likely to be respected and valued. This also makes it easier to check activities against the stated goals.

5. **Agree on a method of conflict resolution up front.** Conflict is inevitable, but it need not be terminal. Differences help to give the facts more depth. The main goal is to deal with the conflict rather than ignore it, and to resolve it if possible and move on.

WHERE DOES THE SERVICE FALL IN THE SERVICE FAMILY HIERARCHY?

Each service you offer is related hierarchically to certain other services your library offers. Your marketing plan introduction should give an indication of where this service fits in with other services you offer. This lays the ground for later sections of the marketing plan that call for you to set goals and objectives for the service.

A service, which may have a brand name, is sometimes part of a *service family*, a group of closely related services. The service family is part of the *service mix*, the set of all services the library offers customers.

The service mix can be described in terms of its length, width, and depth. These concepts are illustrated as a hypothetical example in figure 4-1. In the example, the length of the service mix consists of three service families: Information, Education, and Entertainment. Each service family has several services; this is the width of the family. In the example, the

FIGURE 4-1
Service Mix: Length, Width, and Depth

← Service Mix Length →		
Information	**Education**	**Entertainment**
Reference Collection (5)	Current Topics–Nonfiction (5)	Current Titles–Adult Fiction (5)
In-Library Desk Reference (1)	Nonfiction Author Talks (12)	Adult Fiction Author Talks (12)
Telephone Reference (1)	Basic Literacy Classes (1)	Young Adult Collection (5)
By Appointment Reference (1)	Bibliographic Instruction (2)	Young Adult Programs (12)
E-mail Reference (1)	Research Classes (2)	Children's Collection (5)
Homework Help (1)	Genealogy Resources Classes (1)	Children's Story Hours (2)
Online Chat Reference (1)	Information Literacy Classes (1)	Audio Collection (5)
Business and Career Information (5)	Cultural Awareness Programs (12)	Video Collection (5)
Community Referral Information (20)	Services to School Teachers (2)	
Consumer Information (5)	Introduction to Computer Classes (1)	
Government Information (5)	Internet Search Classes (3)	
	E-mail Classes (3)	

Service Family Width (indicated by vertical arrow on left)

Service depth (the number of variations available) is indicated by the numbers in parentheses. In this hypothetical example, the (3) after Internet Search Classes refers to basic, intermediate, and advanced classes. An actual Current Topics–Nonfiction service would probably have many genres in the collection. In this example we show five, which might refer to books about gardening, finance, health, religion, and pet care.

Education family has twelve services. Finally, each service has variations, which illustrate service depth. In our example, there is one Introduction to Computer class and three Internet Search classes—basic, intermediate, and advanced. The Current Topics–Nonfiction service has five genres—with gardening, finance, health, religion, and pet care titles in the collection. There are twelve Nonfiction Author Talks (one per month).

Various numbers of service variations could be associated with each service in the figure 4-1 example. In constructing your own service mix chart, you would indicate the depth of your services by showing the quantity you offer in parentheses. A state library, regional library, and library consortium with member libraries (customers) would each have a different service mix; for example, the service families might be *acquisitions, collection development, cataloging, reference, interlibrary loan, lobbying,* and *continuing education.*

In setting goals and objectives in the marketing plan, you may decide to lengthen and narrow the service mix, for example, by subdividing the Information, Education, and Entertainment families into Adult, Young Adult, and Children. The result would be a service mix with nine families: Adult Information, Young Adult Information, Children Information, Adult Education, Young Adult Education, Children Education, Adult Entertainment, Young Adult Entertainment, and Children Entertainment. Presumably, each of these families would have fewer services; hence they would be narrower than the currently illustrated three families.

Or you could "prune" the service mix. Instead of the twelve services offered under Education in our example, you might offer nine, eliminating Basic Literacy classes, Cultural Awareness programs, and Genealogy Resources classes. Offering fewer services could save money, free management and staff time and energy, or just allow you to focus better. If you think you need changes to your service mix, address this in developing your goals, objectives, and strategies. Whatever your service mix decisions, each marketing plan should focus on a single service or service family you want to promote.

WHERE IS THE SERVICE IN ITS LIFE CYCLE?

What Is a Life Cycle for a Service?

Every service has a limited life. Like people, services are born (introduced), have a childhood (growth), reach adulthood (mature), and eventually die (decline). Over the course of time, new services come along to displace old services. Early in the nineteenth century, people traveled by horse-drawn wagons, buggies, and stagecoaches. Then railroad and automobile travel displaced these modes of transportation. Now more people opt for airline travel for long distances instead of travel by train or automobile.

A graphed curve—the life cycle curve— is used to illustrate a service as it passes through its different life stages. If you know your service's stage in its life cycle, this knowledge can provide a useful framework for you to develop appropriate strategies to accomplish goals and objectives. The place to discuss your analysis of a service's life cycle stage is the introduction to the marketing plan.

To pinpoint your service's stage, "you have to think big—you have to look at the *overall market,* as indicated by the volume of use of your service and the use of all the major competitors," says Alexander Hiam.[7] For example, in the chat reference services business, you need to look at the volume of use of your own service *plus* those of other libraries and information brokers.

Adapting the Classic Life Cycle for Library Services

The classic life cycle curve, adapted for libraries, is shown in figure 4-2. Note that the volume of service use is plotted as a curve that changes shape from stage to stage. Different strategies work better for different stages, because conditions in each stage are different. The shape of the curve has implications that are important when you begin to develop a strategy. For now, notice that the volume-of-use curve and expense-per-user curve differ. Use is typically low in the introductory stage. The growth stage is characterized as yearly increase in usage. When the service has reached a point where usage is neither growing nor declining, the service has reached the mature stage. The decline stage is characterized by annual decreases in usage. Note that expense per user is highest in the introduction and early growth stages where there are few users to share the high introductory expenses. Expense per user peaks in the growth stage and begins to decline in the mature stage, because expenses are lower after a product is introduced and are shared by a larger number of users. Expense per user begins to rise again in the decline stage, because there are fewer users to share the expense of providing the service.

Your analysis of the overall use patterns of your service should help you determine whether your service is in the introductory, growth, maturity, or decline stage. You may think that when you introduce a new service it is automatically in the introductory stage. If it is sufficiently different from other products or services of its category, maybe it is. However, if it is just new to your library but has been around for a few years or more, it is not in the introductory stage.

FIGURE 4-2
Classic Life Cycle Curve, Adapted for Libraries

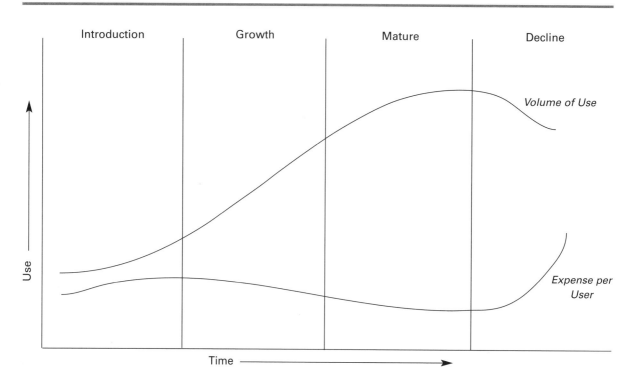

Take, for example, the in-library desk reference service. It has been around for a long time. As a category, in-library desk reference is definitely not in the introductory stage. In fact, with the advent of Internet search engines, use of in-library desk reference by some college students is on the decline. But look at the new virtual reference offerings—e-mail reference and chat reference. They have links on library websites and some services are available 24/7. These are new categories of services in their own life cycles. E-mail reference is an off-site reference service with a time delay, but chat reference is an off-site reference assistance service provided in real time. Chat reference was first made available in 2000. It could be said that this service is in its introductory or early growth stage. On the other hand, e-mail reference service had just entered its growth stage around 2000.

If your library is not offering chat reference or e-mail reference service today, a decision to introduce either service means that service is a new service for your library. The marketing strategies you develop will, however, be different because these two product categories are in different life cycle stages. E-mail reference, which is based on e-mail technology, is familiar to many people. Even senior citizens are familiar with sending an e-mail and getting back a response in a few hours or a few days. Therefore, it may not be difficult to explain and promote the service. In addition, training the users (so that they have a "delightful" experience) should be minimal. On the other hand, chat reference service, which is based on the less familiar instant messaging technology, may come easily only to the younger generation—Gen Xers and teens who use instant messaging frequently. Other customers may need a significant amount of orientation to wait patiently a few seconds (time delay) while the librarian reads the question, types an acknowledgment, then searches for a source for the answer. Your promotional techniques for this service may require the development of educational material as well as material to stimulate use.

Locating Your Service in Its Life Cycle

Designating where each life cycle stage begins and ends is somewhat arbitrary. Usually the stage boundaries are marked where the usage growth or decline becomes pronounced. Worksheet 5 can help you plot the life cycle for your service category. Remember: think big—look at the *overall market*. You state the results of your analysis in the marketing plan introduction, but you will refer to your service's life cycle again when you develop marketing strategies to accomplish your goals and objectives (chapter 7).

SERVICE DESCRIPTION

Now that you thoroughly know your service and you have an idea of how it fits into the one or more target markets you have in mind, you are ready to develop a service description. An effective description of your service should cover the following—what the service is, whom the service is for, and what benefit the service offers to the user.

You are ready to complete section I, Introduction, of the Marketing Plan Template (worksheet 4). Use as much or as little detail as you wish, depending on the purpose of your marketing plan. Figure 4-3 is an example of a completed introduction for chat reference service.

Remember, you have *decided* what the service offer is. But to ensure the success of your service, you should review what you have *discovered* about your target market's needs and wants (see chapter 5), then outline any needed adjustments to your service to "deliver the vision plus one percent" in the marketing plan goals, objectives, and strategies section.[8]

FIGURE 4-3
Service Detail: Completed Worksheet 4, Section I

SECTION I

Introduction

Describe the existing or envisioned service in detail and explain how it fits
into the market:

1. What are the benefits of the service?

   a. What is the core benefit being offered? (What is the customer really seeking?
   What need is the service really satisfying?)

   > To get quick and easy answers to your questions from a person,
   > not a machine.

   b. What benefits accrue to the community/campus when members
   of the target market use this service?

   > High school students who use this service will attain better grades
   > on homework assignments that require research. Better grades on home-
   > work should mean better overall grades, which will allow students to
   > graduate and move on to college or the work world. Eventually they
   > will become literate, productive taxpayers in the community.

2. How are the characteristics of the service managed?

   a. What tangible item(s) does the customer see, feel, hear, touch, or receive
   as a result of receiving this service?

   > Customer sees library web page and the link for chat reference
   > service on his/her computer screen. Customer receives requested
   > information via "pushed" web pages, citations for hardcopy
   > sources, and a transcript of the session.

   b. What library personal does the customer come in contact with to obtain this service?
   What technology does the staff person use to provide this service? How does
   the service function?

   > The librarian assigned to the "virtual" reference desk uses
   > instant messaging technology to provide the service. The customer
   > must have a computer with a modem and access to the Internet.
   > The customer logs on to the library's web page and clicks on the
   > chat reference service, which puts him/her into a real-time ses-
   > sion with a librarian. The librarian assigned to cover the "vir-
   > tual" reference desk for a certain time period is logged on to
   > the web page waiting for someone to enter the chat session.

   c. What steps are being taken to decrease the variability and ensure
   consistent quality when this service is delivered to the customer?

   > All librarians who staff the "virtual" reference desk have two
   > weeks training covering the technology, Internet search engines,
   > content of subscription databases, hardcopy reference sources,
   > and customer service. Librarians also follow a written script
   > for starting and ending the sessions.

   d. What measures are being taken to balance supply and demand for the service?

   > On the supply side: The service will be introduced with limited
   > hours (after school Monday-Friday, 3:00 p.m.–11:00 p.m.) using

part-time staff. On the demand side: English and science teachers in all the high schools in the county will be made aware of the service and the hours of operation. Strategies to increase resources on the supply side and even out demand will be determined after a six-month trial of the service.

   e. What do customers have to do or know to have the best "experience" in seeking the benefits of the service?

Customers must be familiar with computers and be used to participating in online chat sessions.

3. What resources are needed to deliver the service?

   a. What existing or additional hardware, software, electronic databases, print sources, etc., will be used or must be purchased to deliver the service? What staff reallocations or hiring is required?

The library must license instant messaging software and vendor technical and reference service support. Existing licenses for commercial databases, along with web resources and print sources, are sufficient to handle the anticipated informational requests. The modem pool will need to be increased to handle the anticipated additional quantity and length of hits to the website. Existing reference staff will be reallocated to cover service until normal closing at 9:00 p.m. Vendor reference staff will be used to cover time from 9:00 p.m. closing to 11:00 p.m.

   b. What partnerships with other organizations should be forged to supplement or complement capabilities? *(Identify areas to be complemented or supplemented here. Identify potential partners to target and strategies in Sections VI and VII, below.)*

Need to partner with other library systems to provide coverage 24/7.

4. Where does the service fall in the service family hierarchy?

Chat reference will be an addition to the "information" family of services. Will need to determine in the "goals/objectives" section if other services currently being offered in the "information" or other families will be discontinued or de-emphasized. Strategies to accomplish goals/objectives will need to be developed. For example, a widening of the information family (adding a service without discontinuing a service) will require the development of strategies to obtain additional resources.

5. What stage of the life cycle is the service in?

The service is in the introductory stage of the life cycle.

6. What is the service description for your service?

This service allows students who are in need of reference material to get quick and easy answers to their questions from a person, not a machine. All you need is an Internet connection to chat in real time with reference librarians who are able to answer questions and help find resources. You are either provided the specific answers you need or you are directed to the appropriate online and hardcopy resources.

1. Make use of a planning committee to think through all the concepts discussed in this chapter about your service. At a meeting, review service characteristics; how the service functions; what the user has to know; whether you have the needed resources to deliver the product; where the service fits into the service mix; and where it is located in its service life cycle.

2. Don't jump the gun and begin to formulate new strategies. Just review the current information about the service or your vision for the new service.

3. Let the purpose of your marketing plan determine how detailed your introduction, with its description of your service, must be. Plans being used as an internal road map require less written detail; a summary of the information developed in your planning committee could suffice. Plans being used to obtain resources or approval to achieve your goals and objectives require greater detail.

4. If an extensive introduction is not written, keep good notes from your planning committee meeting. This information will be needed for setting goals and objectives and developing strategies and tactics.

NOTES

1. S. B. D. Girvin, *KCLS and UW Virtual Reference Services Marketing Guidelines*, 2002, http://www.secstate.wa.gov/library/libraries/projects/virtualRef/textdocs/MarketingGuidelines.pdf.

2. W. A. Cohen, *The Marketing Plan*, 2d ed. (New York: John Wiley, 1998), 10.

3. K. Blanchard and S. Bowles, *Raving Fans: A Revolutionary Approach to Customer Service* (New York: William Morrow, 1993), 101–102.

4. P. Kotler and A. R. Andreasen, *Strategic Marketing for NonProfit Organizations* (Upper Saddle River, NJ: Prentice-Hall. 1996), 376–383.

5. L. E. Perchetz, "Innovative Partnership Puts Maryland Art Resources Online," The Gazette Online, Johns Hopkins University, Baltimore, 2002, http://www.jhu.edu/~gazette/2002/09sept02/09mdart.html.

6. Adapted from M. Winer and K. Ray, *Collaboration Handbook: Creating, Sustaining and Enjoying the Journey* (St. Paul, MN: Amherst H. Wilder Foundation, 1994), 21–41.

7. A. Hiam, *Marketing for Dummies* (New York: Hungry Minds, 1997), 41–42.

8. Blanchard and Bowles, *Raving Fans*, 101–102.

five

Target Markets

Will the Service Meet Their Needs?

I don't know the key to success, but the key to failure is to try to please everyone.

—Bill Cosby

The University of Louisville libraries used a "market segmentation" approach to increase awareness of their library services. Rae Helton, director of the Office of Information Literacy, and Stuart L. Esrock, assistant professor in the Department of Communications, put their marketing backgrounds to work to develop an "Information Literacy Program" consisting of a variety of research classes tailored to meet the unique needs of students at various levels of preparedness. There are "Jump Start" classes, which offer drop-in mini-sessions designed to cover the basics; a web research class; personal consultation with a reference librarian called "Research One-on-One," and so forth. As Helton and Esrock put it, "Many already know it is not wise to lump together all the potential users of your library and promote services to this mass audience in exactly the same way. . . . The key is to make our library services relevant to each group of potential users. . . . The audiences [target markets] we needed to address were faculty, staff, administration and, of course, 22,000 students. . . . If you think about this situation, it should make perfectly logical sense that what would motivate a student to use the library would be far different than what would motivate a faculty member."

The two went one step farther when they enlisted the students in Esrock's desktop publishing class to provide input about the variety of student needs and their perceptions of the libraries. In addition, these students were assigned the task of designing the logo and promotional materials for the Information Literacy Program. "The creative themes and brochure designs that were presented by the desktop publishing students during finals week were as varied as the student body at U of L. . . . The winning theme spoke to the feelings of information overload expressed by many students." (The library had defined a "harried student" segment as their target market.)[1]

MARKET SEGMENTATION

The process of dividing your entire universe of library users into groups based on common profiles and common wants and needs is called *segmentation*. There are many different ways to group people. The most obvious is to group by demographic criteria such as discussed in chapter 2—ethnicity, age, gender, income, educational level, and the like. People can also be grouped on the basis of lifestyles (psychographic factors) or on how they use the library (usage behavior factors). The objective of segmenting your library users is to find one or more distinct, identifiable groups that are small enough for you to become an expert on their (1) needs for information, educational support, recreation, and entertainment; (2) the competitive alternatives for satisfying their needs; and (3) their communication preferences for being informed about your services.

The premise of segmentation is that the people you group together behave alike when it comes to making decisions about using your service. They are all assumed to have identical or similar needs and to view their competitive alternatives alike. They are exposed to the same media outlets—magazines, newspapers, billboards, TV or radio programs, and so forth. For example, teenagers and seniors are two different target markets that public libraries serve.

Of course, though teenagers are more like other teenagers than they are like seniors, individual teenagers don't all behave alike. This is why marketers seldom use demographics alone to group people. Many marketers have gravitated toward using a combination of demographics with attitude, beliefs, values, and lifestyle factors, which results in statistical clusters of people with similar lifestyles and values—for example, the PRIZM NE segments discussed in chapter 2.

There is also a body of thought, espoused by marketing consultants Don Peppers and Martha Rogers, that the ideal size of a market segment is *one*. In their view, each customer should be treated as an individual. Services should be customized to meet the needs of the individual customer, and promotional materials should be designed with that individual in mind. Furthermore,

> all sampling and projection research is based on predicting *actual* consumer behavior from attitudes and stated intentions. . . . What people say they do and what they actually do are two entirely different things, despite elaborate statistical inference models that use sophisticated analytical tools to try and link the two. The only reliable predictor of *actual* future behavior is *actual* past behavior.[2]

Peppers and Rogers advocate using the power of computers and database technology to store information about all your contacts with your customers—to allow you to provide them customized service. If you are inclined to offer this level of service, you could use your library's circulation system and website to customize your services.

In response to the needs of web-savvy patrons, the Cornell University Library implemented MyLibrary service, making finding and using library resources easier than ever.

MyLibrary allows incredibly detailed targeted marketing of the library's staff, services, and resources. It is an umbrella service for two new products: MyLinks and MyUpdates. MyLinks is a tool for collecting and organizing resources for private use by a patron. The patrons best understand this service as a "traveling set of bookmarks." Most patrons use a variety of machines to access the Internet resources. For example, you may have a computer at home and one at work. Why should you create your bookmarks twice, or carry around a diskette containing your bookmarks? With MyLinks, a patron's favorite sites are just a click away from any machine. MyUpdates helps scholars stay informed of new resources provided by the library. In the past, Cornell University, with its nineteen major library units, addressed this problem by creating accession lists for individual departments. MyUpdates periodically queries the online catalog to determine which resources are new. If the new resources match the pre-identified needs of a patron, the system notifies the patron. Patrons no longer need to search the online catalog regularly to be aware of new resources. MyUpdates searches the online catalog for patrons and e-mails the results to them automatically.[3]

SELECTING THE TARGET MARKET

The selection of a target market (a defined customer group) involves two decisions, about size and characteristics. A marketer can choose a large target market, called *mass marketing*, or a small piece of the market, called *market segmentation*. Although some libraries have begun to practice market segmentation, most public and academic libraries use only the mass market approach, that is, they promote their services to their entire community with one message.

To use scarce promotional resources wisely, however, it is often advisable to narrow the focus to concentrate on the needs of one or two groups in a community. Contrary to the beliefs of some, it is not unfair to target a specific group or groups, even though the library is supported by taxes or tuition from everyone in the user community. Just because you single out a few groups for a specified period of time—to focus your efforts toward meeting their needs and promoting what you have to offer—does not mean you will abandon service to other users in the community. Though you may have fewer items in the collection or fewer staff devoted to these other users, you still have cooperative arrangements with other libraries and information sources to obtain material or information the user is seeking. You just need to ask: What group of people can you reach most effectively? Or what groups are underserved? What service in your service mix (see figure 4-1) meets their needs? How do you promote this service to them? Start by summarizing what you know about your target market(s).

Use section II of worksheet 4, the Marketing Plan Template, to record what you know about your target market. Figure 5-1 is a completed description for the hypothetical teenager market for chat reference service to be offered in a county in Maryland. Using only a few real facts obtained from census reports, the strategic plan for the county's public library, and our own knowledge of the county, we made educated guesses—assumptions about this target market—to fill out this illustration.[4] It is a common practice in business marketing departments for several product managers to get together, review available facts, and make assumptions to fill in the gaps for the marketing plan. In the plan, the assumptions are documented as information from a panel of subject matter experts. The assumptions are always revisited as the plan is executed and actual data become available.

SECTION II

Target Market Description

(Information about the characteristics of your target market may be obtained from a strategic plan or from other worksheets.)

Basic Assumptions *(Record basic assumptions and/or indicate notations used to show that answers to questions 1–10 are assumptions, e.g., with *.)*

> Behavioral data numbers are assumptions. Target market is 17% of total population; assumption is that at least one-third of these teenagers (5.7%) contribute to the library usage figures. Asterick indicates assumption.

1. What are the demographics of the target market?

   What is the size (how many people in total)? 40,867 students in grades 9-12

   Age range: 14–18   Gender: Male _____ Female _____ Both __X__

   Ethnicities: 74.4% white; 20.1% black; 3.2% Asian; 1.8% Latino origin

   Languages spoken:

   > 90.4% English; 2.4% Spanish; 4.4% Indo-European languages; 2.0% Asian & Pacific Island languages

   Income range: Median income: $50,000 (parents' income)

   Education level: 84.3% high school grads; 30.6% bachelor's degree or higher

   Other(s): 50% of teenagers have access to computers at home.*

   What are the significant demographic trends? Population has become more diverse.

2. What are the geographic demographics that have marketing implications for your product/ service? Serving area encompasses 610 sq miles with 26 ZIP codes.

   What is the area's population? 754,292

   What is the population growth pattern (stable, negative, positive)?

   > growing at very slow rate

   How many public and private K–12 schools are in the community?

   > 24 public high schools, 10 private and parochial high schools*

   In what section of the country is the library and its target markets located (North, South, East, West)?

   > In one of 23 counties in one of the Mid-Atlantic states

   What is the population density (urban, suburban, rural)?

   > 610 sq miles with pockets of urban, suburban, and rural communities

   What type of media outlets are available (local, regional, national)?

   > Weekly local community papers; Regional and national daily papers; Regional TV and radio; Local cable outlets; High schools have newspapers; Community organizations have newsletters

   Other(s): _____

3. How do members of this target market use the library (behavioral data)?
   (Categories can overlap. Estimates could exceed 100% of total market size.)

   How many (or what percentage):

   Have library cards?

   > 487,029 total registered borrowers (65% of the population)

   Regularly use the library to borrow materials? 27,760 teenagers*

   Occasionally use the library to borrow materials? 5,000-10,000 teenagers*

   Formerly used the library to borrow materials? None

   Would be first-time library users? 2,000-3,000 teenagers*

   Use materials in the library?

   > 20,000-30,000 teenagers use reference services in the library and online. Very few use telephone reference. 50% have home access to computers.*

   Use reference services?

   > In-library: _____
   >
   > Telephone: _____
   >
   > Online: _____

   Attend library programs? 2,000-3,000 teenagers

   May have never used the library? less than 1,000

4. On what occasions (days of weeks, specific months, holidays) would members of this target market most likely use the service?

   > Chat reference would most likely be used during the school year; Monday-Friday 5:00 p.m. to midnight and Saturday 10:00 a.m. to midnight.* Most use in Oct-Nov; Jan-May.*

5. What are the significant library usage trends?

   > Online visits to website are increasing.

6. What are the five most prominent lifestyles within your target market (psychographics)?
   (Look up by ZIP code "You Are Where You Live" — http://www.yawyl.claritas.com.)

   Lifestyle 1:

   > In ZIP code 21236, segments are all suburban. One with probable teenagers is Home Sweet Home.

   Narrative description:

   > Middle-aged upscale suburbanites; Owner-occupied single-family dwellings; Some college; Professional/white-collar jobs; Lifestyle traits: Go to the movies 4+ times/month; Eat at fast-food burger places; Read Entertainment Weekly; Watch Drew Carey on syndication TV; Drive a Chevy TrailBlazer

   Lifestyle 2:

(cont.)

Gray Power

Narrative description:

Older, middle-class, home-owning suburbanites; High school and
some college; Professional/white-collar jobs. Lifestyle traits:
Go to museums; Own a vacation/weekend home; Watch Live with Regis
and Kelly; Drive a Mercury Sable

Lifestyle 3: _____

Narrative description: _____

_____

_____

Lifestyle 4: _____

Narrative description: _____

_____

_____

Lifestyle 5: _____

Narrative description: _____

_____

_____

7. What are the significant lifestyle trends?

Teenagers emulate the lifestyles of their parents. Lifestyle
traits are those of the middle-class and upscale residents in the
community.

8. What benefits of this service are valued most by members of this target market?
What needs and wants are satisfied by the benefits of this service?

Answers available quickly and easily. Convenience of accessing
Internet from home computer. Ability to get answers at the "11th
hour" before an assignment is due.

9. Why is there a demand for this service in the target market? How much demand is anticipated?

Web-savvy students believe they can get answers to all their
questions by launching a query to an Internet search engine.
They soon realize the search results are not always what they
wanted. They need help getting the "best" search results.
Teachers are also requiring more than web sources for homework.
This service provides reference material from subscription data-
bases, and librarians can direct students to hardcopy sources.
Also, service is available late in the evenings.*

Quantity of Demand (50% of students have home access to computers)*: 10,000-15,000 students use twice a month for 7 months of
the year= 140,000-210,000 sessions a year.* Number of sessions
will grow 10% each year.*

10. What are the media habits of the target market? What type (or specific outlet)

of medium is viewed (e.g., conservative radio talk show; CNN on cable TV)?

```
Students get their information by word of mouth from other
students; Read school newspapers; Get information from school
closed-circuit radio and TV announcements*
```

Medium	Hours/Week	Type (category)
Television	_____	_____
Radio	_____	_____
Magazines	_____	_____
Newspapers	_____	_____

Though the target market described in figure 5-1 is fictional, it is a subset of one of the target markets chosen for a statewide chat reference service in Maryland. The service, AskUsNow!, was officially launched on March 17, 2003. A marketing committee of ten representing several libraries of all types in the state planned the service launch. Joe Thompson, a librarian at the Baltimore County Public Library, chaired the team.[5] The target markets were chosen through discussion and consensus of the team members, who decided to focus on three groups: current public library users, K–12 students in public and private schools, and on-campus and distance education college students. Of secondary priority were five groups: homeschoolers, seniors, special needs users, economically disadvantaged users, and non-users.

In addition to its own experienced knowledge, the committee used data from surveys such as the Pew Internet and American Life Project, which tracks Internet usage. These surveys readily show growing numbers of people who find their information online as well as an increasing demand for online services. "Ideally," Thompson said, "you would want to research specific needs of your desired groups and market to those needs rather than rely heavily on anecdotal experiences."[6]

REVIEWING TARGET MARKET NEEDS AND SERVICE BENEFITS

Now that you have thought about your target market and your service (chapter 4), you can compare the needs and wants of your target market with the benefits of the service you have decided to offer. Do you need to adjust the service to meet your market's needs and wants? Remember, the first two steps in creating raving fans are deciding what you want to offer, and discovering what the customer wants.[7] If you need adjustments, you can document them in the strategies and tactics portion of the marketing plan.

1. Form a marketing committee to act as a panel of subject matter experts.

2. Review your strategic plan and other available data on groups you serve. Discuss and come to a consensus on the target market(s) for your service.

3. Make assumptions, educated guesses, about the data needed on the target market to develop your marketing plan. Thoroughly document your assumptions so they can be revisited as actual data become available when you execute the marketing plan.

4. Review the service benefits and compare them to what you have discovered about the target market's needs and wants. Document any needed changes and address them in the strategies and tactics section of the marketing plan.

NOTES

1. R. Helton and S. Esrock, "Positioning and Marketing Academic Libraries to Students." *Marketing Library Services* 12 (1998), http://www.infotoday.com/mls/apr98/howto.htm.

2. D. Peppers and M. Rogers, *The One to One Future: Building Relationships One Customer at a Time* (New York: Doubleday, 1993), 100–101.

3. Adapted from Suzanne Cohen, John Fereira, et al., "My Library: Personalized Electronic Services in the Cornell University Library," *D-Lib Magazine* 6, no. 4 (2000), http://www.dlib.org/dlib/april00/mistlebauer/04mistlebauer.html.

4. S. Childs, J. Fish, et al., *Strategic Plan VI: Building Community through a Lifetime of Learning* (Towson, MD: Baltimore County Public Library, 2003).

5. J. Thompson, telephone interview, June 3, 2003, on Maryland AskUsNow!

6. Ibid.

7. K. Blanchard and S. Bowles, *Raving Fans: A Revolutionary Approach to Customer Service* (New York: William Morrow, 1993), 101–102.

six

Assessing the Current Marketing Situation

How Does Your Service Stack Up in the Marketplace?

My study of American library history leads me to see information as only a part of a larger library world, in which libraries have done three things especially well for the past century-and-a-half: They have (1) made information accessible to millions of people on many subjects; (2) provided tens of thousands of places where patrons have been able to meet formally as clubs or groups, or informally as citizens. . . ; and (3) furnished billions of reading materials to millions of patrons.

—Wayne A. Wiegand, "Critiquing the Curriculum"

chapter objectives

1. Introduce the concept of the marketing audit.

2. Lead into the chapter on assessing promotional techniques being used to let customers know about the service.

3. Review methods to look at the opportunities available for the service and the issues that may need to be addressed.

A statewide chat reference service—AskUsNow!—was born from an assessment of a trial of chat reference in two counties in Maryland (Baltimore and Harford counties). The trial of chat reference was targeted just to K–12 students. It was envisioned as a service the library could offer to students at "after-school" centers. Joe Thompson and the marketing team referred to lessons learned in this trial as they made plans for the statewide chat reference service offering: "I know going through the planning process of the new service that I referred back to the experience we had with the two-system K–12 oriented service a number of times. We learned such things as where people find out about the service. Our current usage is already confirming what we found then. About 50 percent of people who use the service find out about it simply by seeing it on the library's web page. In other words, it seems they had another reason to go to the library's web page but decided to use the service while they were there. We learned many things in the K–12 targeted service relating to how to staff a service like this, behaviors staff should demonstrate in an online environment, and the general dynamics of an online reference interview. . . . In hindsight [thinking about the two-system K–12 trial], more research should have gone into determining that that group could make use of the service we had developed and wanted to offer. Going into this statewide service, we had the experience to know that the general public and students working from home wanted to use it."[1]

Focusing on the century-and-a-half history of making information accessible to people, librarians in Maryland, and in many states around the country, are assessing the ways technology can be used to meet the information and other needs of their target markets. The Maryland librarians assessed their chat reference trial to determine how effective their efforts were in getting their target market to use the service. They examined everything they were doing from their customer's point of view, paying particular attention to understanding why the customer chooses to use or not use their service given the alternatives from which he has to choose.

THE MARKETING AUDIT

Taking stock of what you are currently doing (or have done in trials) can be as simple as getting your team (your subject matter experts) in a room to brainstorm the answers to some structured questions about the Product (for libraries this is Service) you are offering (or are planning to offer), the Place customers can use it, the Price customers pay to use it, and the Promotional techniques employed to get customers to use it. These are the traditional "4 Ps" of marketing. Another P that has become increasingly important to librarians, however, is Partnerships to supplement or complement the library's resources.

There is one rule to keep in mind when conducting the marketing audit using in-house experts: Examine what you are doing from the point of view of the customer, not from the organization's point of view. How does the customer view your service compared to the alternatives? How does the customer view where the service is offered? How does the customer view the price (time, convenience) required to use the service? How does the customer view your promotional techniques? If your subject matter experts cannot put themselves in the customer's shoes, you should consider hiring a consultant who can employ some market research techniques to find out what your customers think.

QUESTIONS ABOUT SERVICE

In chapter 4 you answered questions about a service's benefits and functionality; you recorded your answers in section I of worksheet 4. But an assessment of your service is not complete until you answer questions about the service's competition, branding, and positioning. Let's look at these now.

What Is Your Service's Competition?

Many librarians have been denying for years that they face a competitive environment. After all, what other entity is in the business of providing *free* books to read and *free* access to information for all? Bookstores charge for their books—so they couldn't be considered competitors . . . right? When bookstores started offering children's story hours, librarians started calling foul: They're stealing our customers; they're competing with us. If bookstores are providing these services, our funding bodies may think they can cut our budget.

Some librarians did recognize the existence of some of their competitors—there are more than bookstores—but they were reluctant to devise marketing plans with strategies to compete with them. After all, the typical librarian might say: Marketing and competing are "not nice" . . . that is what they do in the for-profit world. We are a public resource. We provide service for the good of the public.

In truth, competition is good for the public and the organization. Marketing professors Philip Kotler and Alan Andreasen explain:[2]

> Competition may help rather than hurt the nonprofit marketer's performance in two important ways. First, the existence of two competitors in the marketplace, clamoring for attention, spending two advertising budgets, commanding even more shelf space or media interest, can stimulate increases in the *size of the total market.*

Imagine tremendous increases in the number of children being read to at an early age. These are children who will do well in school and who will grow up to be readers—even library supporters. The entire community benefits from this competition.

> The second way in which competition can benefit the nonprofit is that it can sharpen the competitive skills of the embattled marketers. . . . To compete, they have to rethink how their organization is positioned. They have to look to their customers more carefully to see if there are better ways to meet their needs and wants. They have to consider the possibility of changing offerings, price and advertising.

Competition is defined broadly in a user-centered organization as anything (not just similar products or services) that diverts the customer's attention from your service. Kotler and Andreasen describe four major types of competitor:[3]

Desire competitors. Other immediate desires the consumer might want to satisfy.

Generic competitors. Other basic ways the consumer can satisfy a particular desire.

Service form competitors. Other service forms that can satisfy the consumer's particular desire.

Enterprise competitors. Other enterprises offering the same service form that can satisfy the consumer's particular desire.

An adaptation of Kotler and Andreasen's model is used in figure 6-1 to illustrate these four types of competitors as they are faced by a library chat reference service. A young student evaluates her options for a Saturday afternoon. She realizes that she has several desires she could satisfy: meeting some friends at the mall, getting some exercise, going to a movie, or gathering some information for her term paper. Once she decides to satisfy her *desire* for information, she has to consider various *generic* competitors, including attending a seminar, going to the library, going to the bookstore, or using information sources at home. Choosing to stay at home and obtain information, she has to consider various *forms* of obtaining information—she could make telephone calls and interview sources, watch a TV special, read newspaper and magazine articles, or search the Internet. Finally, after settling on an Internet search, she has to choose among the offerings of various *enterprises*—a self-directed search, asking a friend to come over and help her search, or search with a librarian via the library's chat reference service.

The current marketing situation section of your marketing plan should show that you know who your competitors are at any or all of the four levels of competition. Usually the most intensive competition is at the enterprise level (these are specific companies or products that compete with yours, such as the Main Street Barnes and Noble bookstore or Ask Jeeves). Use worksheet 6, the Service Competitive Audit, to list and assess your competitors at all levels.

Figure 6-2 illustrates an assessment of the competition facing chat reference that could have been developed by librarians in a brainstorming session. At the *desire* level, the choice

FIGURE 6-1

Types of Competitors Facing Chat Reference Service

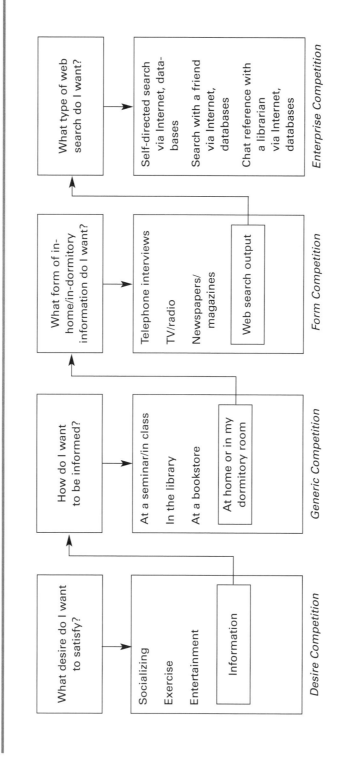

What desire do I want to satisfy?

Socializing

Exercise

Entertainment

Information

Desire Competition

How do I want to be informed?

At a seminar/in class

In the library

At a bookstore

At home or in my dormitory room

Generic Competition

What form of in-home/in-dormitory information do I want?

Telephone interviews

TV/radio

Newspapers/ magazines

Web search output

Form Competition

What type of web search do I want?

Self-directed search via Internet, data-bases

Search with a friend via Internet, databases

Chat reference with a librarian via Internet, databases

Enterprise Competition

Source: Adapted from P. Kotler and A. R. Andreasen, *Strategic Marketing for NonProfit Organizations* (Upper Saddle River, NJ: Prentice-Hall, 1996), 90.

FIGURE 6.2
Competitive Audit: Completed Worksheet 6

List your competitors? How do you rank relative to the competition? Place a "+" to the left of the neutral point to indicate that your service is stronger. The farther left you place it indicates how much stronger it is. Place a "–" to the right of the neutral point to indicate that your service is weaker. The farther right you place it indicates how much weaker it is. List specific company or product names at the Enterprise level.

Desire Alternative	**Competing Alternative:** Gather Information
1. Socializing 2. Exercise 3. Entertainment	Neutral Strong ————————————————— – ———— Weak ———————————————————— – ———— ———————————————————— – ————
Generic Alternative	**Competing Alternative:** At Home/In Dorm
1. Seminar/Class 2. In library 3. Bookstore	Neutral Strong ——— + ———————————————— Weak ———————— + ——————————— —————— + —————————————
Form Alternative	**Competing Alternative:** Web Search
1. Telephone Interviews 2. TV/radio 3. Newspaper/magazine	Neutral Strong ——— + ———————————————— Weak ——— + ———————————————— ——— + ————————————————
Enterprise Alternative	**Competing Alternative:** Chat with Librarian
1. Self-directed search 2. Search with friend 3. _____	Neutral Strong ———————————— – ————— Weak ————————————————— – ——— ————————————————————

Comments: First hurdle to overcome is getting student to think about gathering information for term paper before satisfying other desires. Next hurdle is to get student to realize web search in real-time chat session with a librarian is more productive than searching alone or with a friend.

✓ Goal, Objective, Strategy Checkpoint

How is your service's competitive strength at the Enterprise level?

☐ OK ☑ Adjustment necessary* ☐ Stress in promotion

* Develop goals, objectives, and strategies for adjustments.

of gathering information for a term paper is considerably weaker than the competitive alternatives of meeting friends at the mall, getting some exercise, or going to a movie. Only a sense of obligation or fear of a failing grade would compel our student to choose to seek information for her term paper. At the *generic* level, the choice of staying home and getting information is much stronger than spending money for books at a bookstore and somewhat stronger than going out to class or to the library. At the *form* level, the choice of conducting a web search for information is much stronger than culling through a probably limited collection of newspapers and magazines, much stronger than conducting time-consuming and maybe hard-to-schedule telephone interviews, and much stronger than finding anything of use on TV or radio. At the *enterprise* level, the choice of searching the Internet with a librarian in real time is just slightly weaker than the alternatives of a self-directed search and searching with a friend. Young people are inclined to think that they and their friends know everything and that Internet search engines are infallible.

If this were your service offering and the assessment is correct, you would have to set some competitive goals or objectives and develop strategies to compete with the perceptions young people have about Internet search engines. Use worksheet 6 to assess the competition facing your service.

How Is Your Service Branded and Positioned?

BRANDING

Branding seeks to establish an emotional attachment; it depends on recognition. Branding is the business buzzword of the late 1990s. It is putting a mark (name, logo, typeface) on your service. Al Ries, author of several books on positioning and branding, defines a brand as "a proper noun that can be used in place of a common word. . . . A singular idea or concept that you own inside the mind of the prospect."[4]

Everyone wants to develop a memorable visual symbol of their product, service, or organization that carries an emotional attachment and instant recognition. The golden arches of McDonald's, which originally stood for inexpensive hamburgers served very fast to teenagers of the 1960s, are now recognized by every child as the place to get "happy meals" and possibly a glimpse of Ronald McDonald. The recent introduction of "premium salads" to the menu and a new advertising campaign depicting active young adults is a strategy to extend the brand and reposition it in the minds of more health-conscious adult consumers.

As we enter the twenty-first century, libraries and other nonprofit organizations have seized the concept of branding as a way of getting more recognition for the products and services they offer. Branding, like promotional strategies and tactics, is a quite visible part of marketing. Many libraries and nonprofit organizations, however, have not done the proper homework to develop successful brands.

An exception to this generalization is a library coalition in the state of Washington—the King County Library System (KCLS) and the University of Washington (UW). In their marketing plan guidelines for a virtual reference service, the KCLS/UW coalition wrote: "While many may think a brand springs into life from a single inspiration, in actuality, it takes hard work, focus and commitment. . . . A brand is more than a catchy name, colorful logo or clever ad. A brand includes all of the associations a user makes with the service or product. Successful brands do more than offer tangible benefits. They appeal at a deeper level, evoking an emotional response that endures beyond the initial contact." Two different brands were chosen for virtual reference services offered by the coalition: "School children that use

KCLS are told eAnswer lets you use your computer to 'talk' to and get help from librarians. Undergraduate students at UW are told Q&A Live lets you chat live with librarians and get real-time answers to library related questions through any Web-enabled PC."[5]

POSITIONING

Before you can create that memorable brand, you must first determine your service's position in the mind of your prospect. Robert Gelphman, principal of Gelphman Associates and adjunct professor of marketing at Golden Gate University in California, says, "Positioning is that desirable place in the customer's mind where he not only recognizes the product but he can also recite its attributes."[6]

You have to determine how your target market views your existing service or how they may view your vision of a new service. Do you know what position your service holds in your prospect's mind? Think about the attributes that can be used to describe your service. Can your service be rated superior to your competition on one or more attributes?

In *Positioning: The Battle for Your Mind,* authors Al Reis and Jack Trout say:[7]

> To be successful today, you must touch base with reality. And the only reality that counts is what's already in the prospect's mind. . . . The basic approach of positioning is not to create something new and different, but to manipulate what's already up there in the mind, to retie the connections that already exist.

There are several models to measure the reality of your present position in the prospect's mind. In their book *Strategic Marketing for NonProfit Organizations,* Kotler and Andreasen discuss three of them: Familiarity-Favorability Measurement, Semantic Differential (developed by C. E. Osgood and coworkers in 1957), and Direct Attitude Measurement. In 1985 marketing consultant Chuck McFall introduced Pat Fisher to the Semantic Differential model during a class on effective product management. This useful tool visually depicts the perceptions respondents have about the attributes of a service and its competitive alternatives. It involves several steps, which we describe below and elaborate with our continuing chat reference illustration.[8]

1. *Develop a set of relevant attributes.* The researcher first asks people to identify the attributes they would use in thinking about the object. For example, What things do you think about when you consider a service to help you search the Internet? Presumably, the answer will be a long list of attributes such as "ease of use," "speed of results," user-friendliness of service," "quality of results," and "record of results." Each of these responses is turned into a bipolar adjective scale, with negative adjectives at one end and positive adjectives at the other.

2. *Reduce the set of relevant attributes obtained from step 1.* The number of attributes should be kept small to avoid respondent fatigue in having to rate n services on m scales. Osgood and coworkers proposed three types of scale: Evaluation scales (good–bad qualities), Potency scales (strong–weak qualities), and Activity scales (active–passive qualities).

3. *Administer the instrument to a sample of respondents.* The survey instrument you administer to 100 respondents about chat reference could contain the following questions:

   a. On a scale of 1–5, with 1 being hard and 5 being easy, how would you rate the ease of the following:

      i. Self-directed web search

      ii. Self-directed web search with a friend

      iii. Chat reference with a librarian

b. On a scale of 1–5, with 1 being slow and 5 being fast, how would you rate the speed of obtaining results with the following:

    i. Self-directed web search

    ii. Self-directed web search with a friend

    iii. Chat reference with a librarian

4. *Average the results.* If 75 of 100 respondents rate chat reference on ease of use at 5, and 25 rate chat reference at 4, then the average rating is 4.75, which is rounded to 5. Average the results for each question on the survey instrument for all three services and record the averages in worksheet 7, Semantic Differential. Place a dot on the line between the bipolar adjectives to represent the average rating given each service, and connect the dots. This is a *line of means* for each service.

Figure 6-3 illustrates how worksheet 7 is completed by averaging the perceptions of hypothetical respondents about three web search alternatives. In this example, Chat Reference (alternative C) is seen as an easy-to-use, relatively fast, user-friendly way to get helpful results and a record of websites visited. On the other hand, Self-Directed Web Search (alternative A) is seen as a hard-to-use, relatively slow, unfriendly way of getting a limited amount of useful results with no way of recording websites visited.

FIGURE 6-3

Semantic Differential: Perceptions of Three Internet Search Alternatives

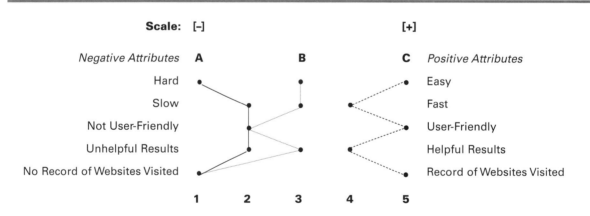

Diagram depicts the average score of three service alternatives on five attributes:

Attribute:	Self-Directed Search (A)	Search w/ Friend (B)	Chat Reference w/ Librarian (C)
Ease of Use:	1 (hard)	3	5 (easy)
Speed:	2 (relatively slow)	3	4 (relatively fast)
User-Friendliness:	2 (not very friendly)	2 (not very friendly)	5 (very friendly)
Quality of results:	2 (not very helpful)	3	4 (pretty helpful)
Record of results:	1 (no record)	1 (no record)	5 (record of websites visited)

5. *Check on the perception variance.* Since each perception profile is a line of means, it does not reveal how variable the perception actually is. If there were 100 respondents, did they all see Self-Directed Web Search, for example, exactly as shown, or was there a little or considerable variation among the respondents? If there was little variation, the perception is highly *specific.* If there was considerable variation, the perception is highly *diffused.* Since the example illustrated in figure 6-3 is hypothetical, we cannot comment on this variance aspect. But in a real case, you would analyze your results from respondents on your bipolar adjective scale to determine if variances are due to different subgroups each having a highly specific perception. For example, do the perceptions of subgroups such as minorities, young adults, or seniors tend to be more alike within their subgroups than when they are averaged with the larger group? If they are—if individuals in each subgroup have similar perceptions—then you want to target the subgroup with the most favorable perceptions of your service. Or you may wish to change some of the aspects of your service to appeal to the subgroups with unfavorable perceptions.

How Does Your Service Fit into the Market?

A positioning map is a useful way of looking at your service compared to other services to determine how it fits into the market. At the enterprise level, select attributes, a pair at a time (two bipolar adjective sets are a pair, e.g., hard/easy and slow/fast), that are the most important to the prospective customer. Use worksheet 8, the Positioning Map, to plot the position of the attributes. Plot them on the *x* and *y* axes to see where they fall in relation to the other attributes and each other. Figure 6-4 illustrates how this is done with the positioning of three alternatives for obtaining information from the Internet.

FIGURE 6-4
Positioning Map of Web Search Alternatives

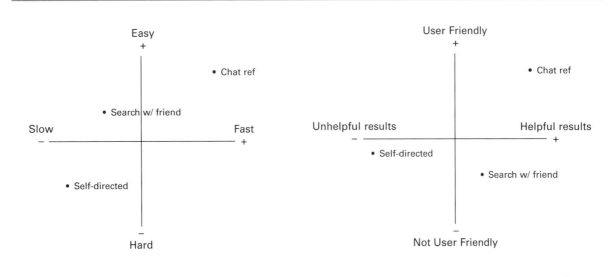

Looking at the positioning map, you can select two or three attributes where your service has a clear competitive advantage and draft a statement that summarizes the "position" the service holds in the prospective customer's mind. This positioning statement should make it easy for people to grasp quickly what type of customer you target, what your service does for the customer, how the service does it, and why the service does it better than the competition.

Continuing with the example of chat reference service, the attributes with clear advantage are *easy*, *user-friendly*, and *helpful results*. In the minds of your prospective customers, "easy," "user-friendly," and "helpful results" already have meaning. You want to retie the connections of these meanings to your service. The positioning statement could read something like: *Chat Reference Service is the easiest way for busy students to get helpful answers online in real time from information specialists, day or night.*

After you complete your assessment of place, price, and promotion, you will be ready to develop goals, objective, strategies, and tactics regarding the building of your brand: you will choose a service name (if you have not already done this), post your positioning statement over your desk, give it to your employees, give it to a graphic artist to create a logo with colors and style that will appeal to your target market, develop a slogan, and so forth.

If your service was the one perceived to be easy, fast, user-friendly, and providing helpful results, it could be assumed that this service has more users than the two competitive alternatives. Therefore, it has the *market leader* position. Your marketing goals, objectives, and strategies will be geared to ensuring that all the elements in the marketing mix (product, place, price, promotion) deliver on the perception of being easy and friendly to use with helpful results. This will ensure retention of the market leader position.

There are four long-term positions an organization might strive for: market leader, market challenger, market follower, and market nicher. Marketing experts suggest different strategy options for each position (see chapter 7).

Record your thoughts about your service's competitive strengths and weaknesses, its position in the mind of prospective customers, and the positioning statement you developed in section III, worksheet 4.

QUESTIONS ABOUT PLACE

Place in marketing means more than the physical location where customers may obtain your service. Your staff and the quality of customer service they provide, as well as barriers to use, atmospherics, and of course location, are all considered important components of place. Although every business knows that the key to success is "location, location, location," many do not know that some libraries have seen circulation of books increase when they are located in retail shopping centers.[9] Place is also referred to as *channels of distribution*—how your services are made available to the customer.

Use section A of worksheet 9, Place and Price Audit, to record the types of outlets where your services are offered. Describe the facilities, noting the positive and negative features and customer reactions.

How Is Your Customer Service Rated by Your Customers?

Library offerings are mostly services. Typically, people produce services, and services are often indistinguishable from the person delivering them. Can your services be considered user-friendly? In today's complicated world, user-friendly is what customers are looking for.

In the business world where many products are becoming commodities, the only way to differentiate products is with outstanding customer service. Often outstanding customer service is obtained when a company decides to prune its mix (see chapter 4 and figure 4-1) so that its staff can focus on delivering a limited number of services.

Are your staff members trained to deliver all your services consistently to all customers? Do you have enough staff and materials to meet the anticipated demand for the services you offer? Do you jettison underused services before offering new services? The thought of removing resources from underused services or discontinuing them when just a few people are still using them may seem like heresy in the library world, but the business world does it every day. Do you supplement your staff with volunteers; how extensive is their training?

How you answer these questions could reveal a lot about the level of customer service you are able to provide. Staff members that are spread too thin cannot be very helpful. Staff members that are not knowledgeable about the collection and other services you provide will not be viewed highly by the customers; they also won't feel very good about themselves. Unhappy staff members make for unhappy customers. Pat Fisher once had a boss who told his managers to practice the "inverted golden rule"—treat your employees the way you want them to treat the customers.

We all know that labor costs are the largest portion of every library's budget. We also know that what keeps people coming to the library is the library's collection of materials. In today's times of stagnate or decreasing budgets, the management challenge to library administrators is how to deliver good customer service cost-effectively.

In the 1990s Pat Fisher served on the board of trustees of the Baltimore County Public Library (BCPL). The library had the reputation of being a no-frills library with good quantities of books people wanted to read and excellent customer service. In fact, its "Give 'Em What They Want" philosophy is what enticed Pat to serve on the board. This philosophy meshed with Pat's philosophy as a marketer: find out what the customer wants and give it to him. Although many of BCPL's administrative practices regarding resources—their purposes, allocation, and uses—were controversial in the library world, they were effective. BCPL is a heavily used library system that prides itself on its staff development practices, its selection of service roles that respond to community needs, and its collection development decisions, among other things.

Are There Barriers to Using Your Products/Services?

Using your services should be as convenient and barrier-free as possible. Barriers may be related to hours of operation, parking, accessibility by public transportation, neighborhood safety, lending policies for reference material, policies on fines and fees, or availability of Internet access. You should examine the barriers to use of each service you offer from the point of view of your target market.

The librarians in Baltimore and Hartford counties in Maryland realized their service had barriers during a trial of a chat reference service. They had received a Library Services Technology Act grant to conduct the trial. The barriers-to-use challenges they encountered with their initial target market led them to target a different market when they launched the service statewide. Baltimore County librarian Joe Thompson said that "the grant was geared to working with students at after-school centers, which was an enormous challenge (in some ways more than just operating a virtual reference service to all). . . . Throughout that year [of the trial], I kept having the sensation of roadblock after roadblock while after-school centers tried to get access to the Internet."[10]

When evaluating place, also look for things that could be an advantage; you may have something to tout in your promotional efforts. For example, your location could be in a particularly convenient spot or near a special attraction. Your distribution method might be delivery by fax, by courier (books via UPS), or web pages "pushed" to your home computer.

What Are the Atmospherics Associated with Your Services?

Atmospherics refers to the intentional design of the place of delivery to create or reinforce specific effects on buyers, such as feelings of well-being, safety, intimacy, or awe. The atmospherics of a particular place may add or detract from consumer satisfaction and employee performance. The latter point deserves special emphasis. Since the employees work in the facility all day long, the facility should be designed to support them in performing their work with ease and cheerfulness.

Though many think this aspect of place comes into play only when you are designing a library for the first time or embarking on a large remodeling project, atmospherics can also be a major factor in a variety of other situations: a story hour service for toddlers and their caregivers; a teen poetry writing program; an adult book discussion club; a web page service for senior citizens; a reference-by-appointment service for college students. Aside from the obvious considerations of what the facility should look like on the outside and what the functional and flow characteristics of the inside should be, there is a great depth of other characteristics that go into creating an atmosphere. Kotler and Andreasen use an example of the construction of a new art museum to mention some of them:[11]

> What should the museum *feel* like on the inside? Every building conveys a feeling, whether intended or unplanned. The planners have to consider whether the museum should be awesome and somber, bright and modern, or warm and intimate. Each feeling will have a different effect on the visitors and their overall satisfaction. . . .
>
> What materials would best support the desired feeling of the building? The feeling of the building is conveyed by visual cues (color, brightness, size, shapes), aural cues (volume, pitch), olfactory cues (scent, freshness), and tactile cues (softness, smoothness, temperatures). The museum's planners have to choose colors, fabrics and furnishings that create or reinforce the desired feeling.

The Richmond Public Library in British Columbia understands the role atmospherics can play in customer satisfaction and employee performance. Their Ironwood branch beckons customers to come on in and stay a while. The most heavily used room in the Ironwood branch is called the "living room." It has a corner reading area, river-rock fireplace, and comfortable chairs. There are attractive wooden display carts of CDs with listening stations. Books are arranged in large and ever-changing displays, which are everywhere. Customers can relax in the living room with food, drink, and books. Library staff circulate through the library to assist customers rather than wait to be approached at the desk. "We want visitors to come on in and enjoy themselves," says Cate McNeely, deputy chief librarian and Ironwood project manager. . . . "We designed this library to give customers what they want—an inviting atmosphere, friendly knowledgeable staff walking the floor and providing assistance, merchandized collections, convenient and longer hours, personalized service via our website and more. . . . I think we can all agree that reading a book is a wonderful, exciting and often joyous experience. Unfortunately public library buildings do not always evoke that same wonder and excitement. At Richmond Public Library, we want our customers' library experience to reflect that sense of fun and excitement. So instead of coming into a conservatively designed space, our customers arrive into an exciting environment that is full of energy and invites exploration."[12]

QUESTIONS ABOUT PRICE

Library administrators and governing boards must make decisions about what to offer, how to offer, and where to offer services to meet the needs of the majority of the potential users in the community. When you can show funding bodies that the services you offer are efficiently meeting the needs of those they represent, that the services are heavily used, that the services are generating specific social benefits to the community, and that your constituents want their tax or tuition dollars to support the library, the library's budget tends to be adequate—barring economic downturns, of course. For the most part, communities get the library services they are willing to pay for.

This is also true in the business world. Businesses must consider what their target market is willing to pay to receive the benefits of their products and services. If what the target market is willing to pay does not cover the cost—plus provide some profit—the features and functionality of a product or service may need to be altered to reduce its costs: It may need to be a Chevrolet instead of a Cadillac; it may need to be offered to a different target market that is willing to pay more, or it may need to be not offered at all.

To get the members of your community to use library services—and thereby show funding bodies that your services are needed and wanted—you must offer potential users something that meets their needs at a price they are willing to pay.

The library user may pay in the form of time or convenience as well as other psychological costs such as intimidation or frustration. For example, users frequently must wait to obtain materials they want to borrow as opposed to going to a bookstore to make an immediate purchase. It could be that they wait in some queue to borrow a copy of a popular best seller because it is in great demand. They could even wait to borrow material that has normal demand. If the material is newly purchased, it has to be cataloged, labeled, and shelved before it can be circulated. Returned material may have to be mended before it is reshelved. Material not owned by a particular library—or branch—must be requested via interlibrary loan. In many libraries, staff is limited, which causes backlogs in getting material on shelves.

Users of library information services may also experience psychological costs, as described by Elizabeth Wood:[13]

> Mature patrons [who are] competent in most areas of their lives, [may be intimidated by librarians, therefore] they can be reluctant to ask questions or to confess to unfamiliarity with the layout or procedures of the library . . . frustration [is] suffered by patrons when a librarian who has not done good question negotiation not only wastes time on peripheral issues, but also ultimately fails to answer questions central to their [patron's] information needs.

The price issue librarians are most sensitive about is fees—late fees, reserve fees, and others—to use library services. Wood acknowledges that fees are controversial and hotly debated within the profession. "Some of the hottest debate has been and will continue to be centered on the issue of whether fees are ever justified. Ideally, fees should never be a barrier to use; everyone deserves equal, unrestricted access to information."[14] On the other hand, fees can give libraries the ability to provide value-added services on a cost-recovery basis. Some services, for example, copy machine and printing access, would not likely be made available if fees were not allowed to cover the cost of providing the services.

Another psychological aspect of price is what customers perceive they are getting based on the price they pay. Many people believe that anything that is free is not valuable, that items with a higher price tag are of better quality, and that items with a lower price tag are of lesser quality.

Library administrators and governing boards can employ collection development and staff development practices and fee policies that minimize these costs for prospective users. They should also find ways to let library users know the value of their library services. For example, displays in the library or items that can be distributed (fact cards, bookmarks) might contain comparisons such as "500,000 books were borrowed from the library. At a cost of $25 per book, this would have cost taxpayers in the community $12.5 million."

Library users may also be required to have certain equipment to use certain library services. For example: VCR/DVD players are required to use any tapes or DVDs that are borrowed; a computer with Internet access is required to use online reference services remotely. If customers cannot pay the price to buy this equipment, they cannot use these services.

The service benefits, the place issues such as customer service and atmospherics, and the competitive alternatives all determine if users are willing to pay the costs to obtain services from the library.

Record your thoughts on questions about price in section B of worksheet 9 and section III of worksheet 4.

QUESTIONS ABOUT PROMOTION

Flyers, bookmarks, magnets, mugs, and other promotional material are the most visible signs of efforts to make users and non-users aware of your library or specific services your library has to offer. For this reason, many librarians think that conducting promotional efforts is marketing. We hope you have come to understand that marketing is much more than promotion. Again, marketing is the analysis and planning process required to facilitate exchanges of something of value for something wanted or needed. Creating a promotional campaign is the last step in marketing. Promotion covers all the ways you communicate with existing and potential customers. It includes the broad categories of sales, advertising, public relations, and a long list of specific techniques—from brochures to the annual holiday open house to public service announcements on the radio. To do justice to the discussion of assessing this important P of the marketing mix, we addressed it separately in chapter 8.

OPPORTUNITY AND ISSUE ANALYSIS

The marketing plan's opportunity and issue analysis section is a summary that emphasizes the main points you have already covered in preceding sections. You may be more familiar with this analysis being referred to as a SWOT (Strengths, Weaknesses, Opportunity, and Threats) analysis. As you analyzed your service offering, described your target market, and conducted the marketing audit, you covered many of the competitive strengths, weaknesses, and threats facing your service offering. These analyses also provided you insight into the opportunities and issues (threats) that confront your service offering.

In section IV of worksheet 4, restate the opportunities and issues explicitly, listing them one by one. Group them first by opportunities, then by issues. Indicate why each is an opportunity or an issue. Also indicate how you intend to take advantage of each opportunity and what you intend to do about each issue.

1. Convene a panel of subject matter experts to conduct the marketing audit:

   a. Review the service's competitive positioning in the target market.

   b. Discuss the implications the target market's perceptions of the service can have on branding decisions: choice of name, color, design.

   c. Discuss the questions about place: barriers to use, atmospherics, customer service.

   d. Discuss the questions about price: community's willingness to pay and customer willingness to pay.

   e. Discuss opportunities and issues facing the service.

2. Document the audit by completing the worksheets. Use information in the worksheets to write the appropriate narration for the marketing plan. Also, use the information to formulate the Goals, Objectives, and Strategy sections of the marketing plan.

NOTES

1. J. Thompson, telephone interview, June 3, 2003, on Maryland AskUsNow!

2. P. Kotler and A. R. Andreasen, *Strategic Marketing for NonProfit Organizations* (Upper Saddle River, NJ: Prentice-Hall, 1996), 88–91.

3. Ibid., 89–90.

4. A. Ries and L. Ries, *The 22 Immutable Laws of Branding: How to Build a Product or Service into a World-Class Brand* (New York: HarperCollins, 1998), 172.

5. S. B. D. Girvin, *KCLS and UW Virtual Reference Services Marketing Guidelines*, 2002, http://www.secstate.wa.gov/library/libraries/projects/virtualRef/textdocs/MarketingGuidelines.pdf.

6. R. Gelphman, "Every Company's Marketing Goal: To Be Known and Wanted," *San Jose Business Journal*, April 5, 2002, p. 12.

7. A. Ries and J. Trout, *Positioning: The Battle for Your Mind* (New York: McGraw-Hill, 1982), 5.

8. This outline of semantic differential steps is drawn from Kotler and Andreasen, *Strategic Marketing for NonProfit Organizations*, 190–191.

9. Baltimore County Public Library's Blue Ribbon Committee, *Give 'Em What They Want! Managing the Public's Library* (Chicago: American Library Association, 1992).

10. J. Thompson, telephone interview, June 3, 2003, on Maryland AskUsNow!

11. Kotler and Andreasen, *Strategic Marketing for NonProfit Organizations*, 464–465.

12. Cate McNeely, personal interview, March 17, 2005.

13. E. J. Wood, with assistance from V. L. Young, *Strategic Marketing for Libraries: A Handbook* (Westport, CT: Greenwood Press, 1988), 72–73.

14. Ibid., 71.

Setting Goals and Objectives with Supporting Strategies

The Art of Focusing Your Resources

> "Cheshire Puss," [Alice] began . . . "would you please tell me which way I ought to go from here?"
>
> "That depends on where you want to get to," said the cat.
>
> —Lewis Carroll, *Alice in Wonderland*

chapter objectives

1. Discuss goal and objective setting.
2. Explore the different levels of marketing strategy, which include core marketing strategy, market position strategy, product life cycle strategy, and marketing mix strategy.

A ten-year strategic plan of the Maryland State Department of Education, Division of Library Development and Services, contained a broad strategic directive: help to increase public awareness of library services. To carry out this directive, a marketing task force composed of twenty-seven individuals from around the state was formed. The task force (1) selected a target market that was served by all the public libraries in the state—children from birth to five and their parents and caregivers; and (2) established goals for a marketing plan: increase the public's awareness of library services for young children; increase library staff's knowledge and skills to serve young children, their parents, and caregivers; and increase the community resources and support for services to children ages birth to five.

A subset of the task force, a steering committee led by Marcy Pride, was commissioned to develop and execute a public awareness campaign—It's Never Too Early—for the library services that met the needs of this target market. In the public awareness campaign, story times for infants and toddlers and take-home story kits (age-appropriate books, puppets, and reading-aloud tips for parents and caregivers) were positioned as a solution to the school system's low scores on tests, and libraries were positioned as the only place offering story times for infants and toddlers from trained professionals. The campaign's objectives spelled out measurable milestones, and the marketing mix—product, price, place, promotion—strategies and tactics accomplished the campaign's goals. The campaign won the John Cotton Dana award and landed the state superintendent of education and libraries an invitation to First Lady Laura Bush's White House conference on emerging literacy.[1]

66

The Maryland public libraries knew where they wanted to go, and their plan took them there. They adopted a core marketing strategy of *differentiation* to get them there. What they had to offer was trained professionals reading books to children and engaging them in songs and finger-play versus bookstore personnel reading to children.

GOALS AND OBJECTIVES

As the vignette about Maryland public libraries illustrates, marketing goals, objectives, a core marketing strategy, a positioning strategy, and marketing mix strategies help you focus your limited resources on a path that benefits your community, help you show your value to key stakeholders. and maybe get you more resources.

We authors have come from different environments where the terms *goal* and *objective* have been used differently. In fact, many people use these terms interchangeably. For the purposes of this book, however, we define goals to be broader in nature. Goals relate to the endgame you are trying to achieve over the planning horizon. The planning horizon is normally the same as the period of time covered by your strategic plan. Objectives, on the other hand, we define as measurable, achievable milestones; they are the means of quantifying your goals; they set specific dates and numbers for growth or for decreases, for example.

The process of defining your endgame (goals) and setting measurable and attainable milestones (objectives) requires you to determine what resources you need to be successful. You have to focus your resources—staff, materials, budget—to attain your goals and objectives. Depending on the amount of resources at your disposal, you may have to divert resources from other activities, or you may have to acquire additional resources.

Setting Goals

Ideally, goals are based on the strategic directions from your strategic plan.[2] Goals should do most of the following:

> Support the library's basic purpose.
>
> Clearly state what the endgame will look like, preferably by a certain time period or date.
>
> Be obtainable; if they cannot be obtained, they will motivate no one.
>
> Be acceptable to those who will make the decisions to allocate resources to implement your marketing plan.
>
> Be flexible enough to be modified in the event of unforeseen contingencies or environmental changes.
>
> Elicit acceptance from those who will be working on the development, planning, and execution of the marketing plan.

Examples of common goals libraries adopt are increasing awareness, usage, staff knowledge and skills, and library funding. The following goal may have been set by the librarians who developed the chat reference service we have been using as an example throughout this book:

> *Goal:* Develop a service for teenagers that will increase the usage of the library's website over the three-year planning horizon.

Worksheet 10, Goals, Objectives, and Strategies, is available to record your goals. Use one worksheet for each goal. The next step in the marketing planning process is to create objectives to clarify your goals with measurements. Worksheet 10 accommodates several objectives for each goal.

Creating Objectives

Remember that objectives are the means of quantifying your goal. For the goal stated above, the objectives should specify (1) what the new service to be developed is, (2) how much of an increase is desired, and (3) when the increase should be reached. The following could be objectives for the goal:

Objective 1: Provide a real-time chat reference service, accessed via the library's website, which can be tested by teenagers in year 1 of the planning horizon.

Objective 2: Increase teenagers' use of the library's website by 10 percent a year for years 2 and 3 of the planning horizon.

Now you need to develop strategies to accomplish the objectives. Worksheet 10 accommodates several strategies to implement the goal and objectives.

MARKETING STRATEGIES

Simply put, strategy is the "why and how" of what you want to do. Strategy is an organized idea of how to accomplish your goals and objectives. The word *strategy* stems from the Greek *strategos*, which means the "art of the general." Many of the concepts used in marketing strategy evolved from early use in military strategy. The strategies, which range from the general (grand strategy) to the specific (tactics), clearly illustrate the phrase "to drill down."

What Are the Levels of Strategy in Marketing Planning?

The levels of military strategy, as they may be applied to marketing planning in libraries, are illustrated in figure 7-1. The grand strategy for libraries is articulated in *strategic directives*,

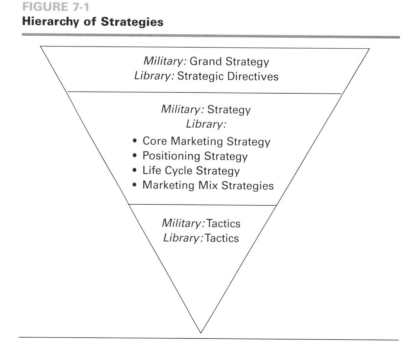

FIGURE 7-1
Hierarchy of Strategies

Military: Grand Strategy
Library: Strategic Directives

Military: Strategy
Library:
- Core Marketing Strategy
- Positioning Strategy
- Life Cycle Strategy
- Marketing Mix Strategies

Military: Tactics
Library: Tactics

the goals and objectives of the strategic plan. The next level of strategy concentrates on developing a core marketing strategy and a positioning strategy. According to Philip Kotler and Alan R. Andreasen, the single most important stage in the strategic marketing planning process is determining the organization's core marketing strategy, which has three elements:[3]

1. One or more specific target markets

2. A clearly defined competitive position

3. A carefully designed and coordinated marketing mix to meet the needs of the target markets while differentiating the product/service or organization from major competitors

There are three basic core strategies an organization can adopt:[4]

1. *Differentiation.* In this approach something is offered that no or few other competitors can offer, in terms of real differences or perceived differences.

2. *Cost leadership.* This approach involves marketing the lowest-cost offerings in the marketplace. "Free" is not necessarily the lowest-cost offering. Time consumption and lack of convenience are costs.

3. *Focus.* In this approach a limited segment of the market is selected—typically one not served by anyone else in the market—and concentrated on in order to serve that market uniquely.

Adopting any one of the three core strategies allows you to create a position in the marketplace. As Regis McKenna writes in *The Regis Touch*, "All marketing strategies—product, packaging, price, place, promotion, public relations [and partnership]—grow out of positioning."[5]

Market Position Strategies

When you evaluated your current marketing situation (chapter 6), you conducted an exercise to determine your service's competitive position in your target market's mind. Market positions, and their appropriate strategies, discussed in this chapter are based on the work of Kotler and Andreasen.[6] If your prospective customer considers your service to have attributes similar to those of one or two other competitive services, the service with the most users—considering the total market— is the *market leader*. The services with similar attributes but fewer users are either *market challengers* or *market followers*. A service that is not in the introductory phase of its life cycle, has no competitors, and has unique attributes valued by a small target market has a *market niche*. Whatever your market position, if prospective customers perceive your service to be "best" or "superior" on any attribute, then that is the attribute you promote. In the car rental business, Hertz is the market leader by virtue of having more customers (more market share). Avis, the market challenger, has similar attributes and may be perceived as just a little lower in cost; it promotes itself with "We are #2. We try harder." Prospective customers are intended to understand trying harder as having better customer service.

MARKET LEADERS

Leaders want to continue having more customers than their competitors. They employ strategies that expand total demand for their service and protect their market share. In general, when total demand increases, market leaders stand to gain the most. Assuming that the library is the market leader for chat reference, the three ways to expand demand are obtaining new users, discovering new uses, and increasing usage:

Obtaining New Users. Persuade more people in the target market to use the service. This is a market penetration strategy. In the ongoing chat reference example, the target market is teenagers in a specific county in Maryland. If 25 percent of the teenagers in the market use the service, convince some of the 75 percent who don't use the service to become users.

Persuade people in other markets to use the service. This is a *new market strategy.* New target markets for chat reference could be college students or senior citizens, for example.

Determine if there are parts of your serving area where you have not offered the service. This is a *geographic expansion strategy.* This strategy is not applicable in the ongoing chat reference example because the service was offered to all teenagers in the serving area when it was introduced. If it had been offered to only part of the serving area when introduced, this would be a viable strategy.

Discovering New Uses. Look for new ways to use the service, and promote the new use to customers in the current target market. For example, baking soda's original use was baking; it is now promoted as a freshener for refrigerators. In the chat reference example, the original use for teenagers is general homework help. A new use could be specific help in compiling bibliographies for term papers.

Increasing the Usage. Persuade current users to use more of the services you offer each time they visit. For example, if users access chat reference from the library's home page, get them also to access electronic databases from the home page. Advertise programs that appeal to the target market, and get users to sign up from the home page; get them to reserve books from the home page.

Leaders must continuously protect against competitive attacks. Leaders apply the military principle that the best defense is a good offense by exercising initiative, setting the pace, and exploiting the weaknesses of competitors. Two ways to protect market share are practicing continuous innovation and plugging service voids:

Practice Continuous Innovation. Leaders constantly look for new service ideas; improvements to services, customer service, and the place the service is obtained; and ways to cut costs. For example, libraries have been the leading source of information services for decades. To keep a market leader position, libraries have embraced technology to offer information services in the library and from remote locations.

Plug Service Voids. Leaders supply services to niche markets to satisfy their needs, especially when services are not being offered (or promoted) by competitors. For example, libraries provide books recorded on tape or disc for commuters and those with sight impairment.

MARKET CHALLENGERS

Challengers employ strategies to take customers away from the leader. Assuming that the library is the market challenger for some specific services, with the market leaders being bookstores, senior citizen centers, and other organizations, any of several strategies could be employed by the library to take customers away:

Cost Discount Strategy. Attract customers with service offerings that are comparable to the leader's services at a lower cost (economic, psychological). For example, best sellers can be obtained from libraries for a lower economic cost (free or small reserve fee), though the psychological cost may be higher; customers may wait in a queue to obtain the book, and they have a limited time to use the book.

Cheaper Goods Strategy. Offer the market a lower-quality service than the competitor's at a lower cost. An example might be used books at low prices.

Prestige Goods Strategy. Offer a higher-quality service and charge a higher price than the leader. One-on-one research assistance with a reference librarian by appointment is an example. The price: a long wait for appointments.

Service Proliferation Strategy. Offer the market a larger number of services than the leader. For example, offer senior citizens more activities to do in the library than can be found in senior centers.

Service Innovation Strategy. Find a way to take a more novel approach to offering services to your customers. For example, welcome them to your library with a neon sign that says Welcome in many languages.

Improved Services Strategy. Find ways to offer new or better services to customers. Professional librarians offering reader's advisories might provide better service than bookstore clerks, for example.

Distribution Innovation Strategy. Discover or develop new places to offer the service. Offer a "new baby kit" comprising books, reading tips, and a list of library services at hospitals.

Intensive Advertising and Promotion Strategy. Attack the leader by increasing expenditures on advertising and promotion. This is not a sensible strategy unless the challenger's service or advertising is distinctive or superior to the leader's service or advertising. In the library's case, spending money on advertising is rare. However, library services like story times for infants and toddlers are superior services that could be intensely promoted. Many libraries are using ideas generated from the American Library Association's @ your library campaign, along with ideas and promotional material templates from vendors such as Thompson-Gale and 3M to promote their offerings. See chapter 8 for promotional techniques.

MARKET FOLLOWERS

Followers are content to employ strategies to hold their current customers and obtain new customers as markets grow without competing head-to-head with the leader. Assuming that the bookstore is the market leader and the library is the follower, the library could employ these strategies:

Follow the Leader Closely. Emulate the leader in as many market segments and marketing mix elements (product, price, place, and promotion) as possible. A public library that chooses the "current topics and titles" role may carry large quantities of best sellers and provide author talks. They may have inviting, attractive interiors with merchandise displays, cafés, and the like.

Follow the Leader at a Distance. Emulate the leader in just the major market innovations and distribution channels (outlets or place). For example, a library might choose to create inviting displays of its collection while not concentrating on best sellers and not offering author talks.

Follow the Leader Selectively. Emulate the leader in some aspects, go your own way in others. A library might emulate the leader in providing children's books while surpassing the leader in providing programming for children such as story times or arts and crafts programs.

MARKET NICHERS

Nichers employ specialization strategies that avoid clashes with major competitors. Many nichers practice a multiple niching strategy. Assuming that the library wanted to provide services to market niches, it might employ these strategies:

End-Use Specialist. The library specializes in serving one type of end-use customer, for example, medical students, law students, business students, local historians, or genealogists.

Customer-Size Specialist. The library limits its "Business and Career Information" service role to providing services and collection materials that benefit small businesses and entrepreneurs.

Service-Feature Specialist. The library specializes in providing a certain type of service, such as access to government documents.

Service Specialist. The library offers one or more services not readily available from other firms, such as telephone and chat reference or books on tape.

Service Life Cycle Strategies

Although the assessment of your library's market position may be valuable in helping you determine strategies and subsequent tactics to use in your marketing planning, the stage of your service's life cycle may also suggest strategies to accomplish your goals and objectives.[7]

Introductory Stage Strategies. The introductory stage requires a strategy to establish market share, which is a *pioneering strategy*. You are venturing into new territory for your customers and your staff. Basically, you want to get as many customers as you can, and you want to persuade early adopters—people who are always on the cutting edge and willing to try new things—to try your service. This may require educating your customers on the use and advantages of the new service. This may also require strengthening the place where the service is offered—by educating your staff on how to deliver the service, thus enhancing customer service; by removing barriers to use; and by enhancing atmospherics. There are few, if any, competitors in this stage. Customers tend to be loyal to the first providers of a service. Tactical support of a pioneering strategy includes trial usage offers and service demonstrations.

Growth Stage Strategies. The growth stage requires a strategy to penetrate new markets, which is a *competitive strategy*. Early adopters in your target market have already accepted the service and no longer need much education about it. Customers in new markets may be sought. By this time, however, many more competitors have entered the market. You protect your market share by exercising initiative, setting the pace, and exploiting the weaknesses of your competitors. Tactical support of a competitive strategy includes service improvement, development of new places to obtain the service, and manipulation of price and quality.

Maturity Stage Strategies. The maturity stage requires an entrenchment (digging in) strategy, which is a *retentive strategy*. Your service has been around a while, and it can be obtained from a variety of competitors. The market is becoming saturated. You may need to fight your competitors to keep your customers. Your strategies for retaining customers could include building relationships with your customers—this encourages loyalty—and making improvements to the service and other elements of the marketing mix, customer service and atmospherics, for example. Or you could reposition the service to appeal to different markets with less competition. Tactical support for a retentive strategy includes reducing the number of places the service is available to reduce costs, reducing the costs (economic and psychological) to the customer, and increasing emphasis on promotion.

Decline Stage Strategies. The decline stage requires a *withdrawal* or *repositioning strategy*. In this stage, very few people are using the service, and very few, if any, competitors are providing the service. You need to plan to stop offering the service or reposition it. The mildest form of withdrawal is to decrease the number of places and number of hours the service is offered gradually until you have fewer and fewer users. Of course, you could just stop offering the service without a gradual decrease in availability, reallocating your resources to provide services that are in higher demand. Repositioning requires changing the service or its uses to appeal to a different market.

MARKETING MIX STRATEGIES
FOR THE MARKETING PLAN

Now it is time to combine what you know about market position strategies and service life cycle strategies with what you know about your target market and your current marketing situation from the marketing audit to form the strategies to accomplish your goals and objectives. Remember, strategies tell "how and why" you are doing something to accomplish goals and objectives. Let's look at each element of the marketing mix.

Service (Product) Strategies

Review worksheets and the sections of the marketing plan template that address your assessments of your service and your target market. Your assessment should suggest several strategies. Your choice of strategies also determines the tactics you implement to achieve your goals and objectives.

For example, the service we have been using as an example throughout this book, chat reference, is in the introductory stage of its life cycle. Its benefits of providing quick and easy answers from a person, not a machine, match the needs of the target market. It has a strong competitive position in the mind of the prospective customers. The service has more users than competitors. The library offering is the market leader. The following service strategy could be employed to accomplish the sample goal and objectives listed in this chapter:

Strategy 1: Provide demonstrations on how to use chat reference for one year at the various middle schools and high schools in the area to familiarize students and teachers. (Educating the customer is a *pioneering strategy.*)

Place Strategies

Review your place audit worksheet (worksheet 9). Continuing with the chat reference example, the following place strategies could be employed to accomplish the sample goal and objectives listed in this chapter:

Strategy 2: Collaborate with other library systems and a vendor who provides reference staff for virtual desk coverage twenty-four hours a day, seven days a week, via the library's website to make the service available any time it is needed by teenagers.

Strategy 3: Develop an online interview script for reference librarians and provide them with at least one week of training on interview behaviors required in an online environment to ensure consistent quality of service.

Strategy 4: Place the distinctive logo (brand) for the chat reference service in a prominent place on the library's home page and on the teen page of the library's website so that teens can readily access the service.

Price Strategies

Review your price audit worksheet (worksheet 9). Continuing with the chat reference example, the following price strategy could be employed to accomplish the sample goal and objectives listed in this chapter:

Strategy 5: Monitor the website access statistics to ensure that all attempts to click on to the chat reference service are connected to a reference librarian within three seconds to eliminate any perceived inconvenience costs.

Promotion Strategies

As you can see from reading the preceding chapters, promotion is the last step in developing the marketing plan. Your promotional strategy may call for a small-scale promotional campaign that can be executed in-house with minimal, if any, outside graphic design or professional writing support. Or your promotional strategy may call for a large-scale promotional campaign requiring graphic designers, writers, or other communications professionals such as public relations firms. Since this is such a visible part of your marketing plan, we devote chapter 8 to discussions of the topics of assessing your current promotional techniques and developing promotional strategies to accomplish your goals and objectives.

Developing the tactics (tasks) and budgets to carry out your strategies are discussed in chapter 9.

quick-start tips

1. Convene a panel of subject matter experts to review the worksheets you have completed about your service, your target market, your competitive position, and your marketing audit of the marketing mix elements.

2. Use worksheet 10 (one for each goal) to list your goals, objectives, and strategies.

NOTES

1. M. Pride, "How to Market Your Library," presentation to the Black Caucus of the American Library Association," Ft. Lauderdale, FL, August 15, 2002.
2. The section based on points listed in W. A. Cohen, *The Marketing Plan*, 2d ed. (New York: John Wiley, 1998), 32–38.
3. P. Kotler and A. R. Andreasen, *Strategic Marketing for NonProfit Organizations* (Upper Saddle River, NJ: Prentice-Hall, 1996), 150.
4. Ibid., 151–152. Kotler and Andreasen credit these points to M. Porter, *Competitive Strategy: Techniques for Analyzing Industries and Competitors* (New York: Free Press, 1980).
5. R. McKenna, *The Regis Touch* (Reading, MA: Addison-Wesley, 1991), 14.
6. This section based on Kotler and Andreasen, *Strategic Marketing for NonProfit Organizations*, 192–203.
7. This section based on Cohen, *Marketing Plan*, 54–60.

eight

Promotion

Assessment, Goals, Objectives, and Strategies

If the circus is coming to town and you paint a sign saying "Circus Coming to the Fairground Saturday," that's advertising. If you put the sign on the back of an elephant and walk him into town, that's promotion. If the elephant walks through the mayor's flowerbed, that's publicity. And if you get the mayor to laugh about it, that's public relations.

—Lisa Wolfe, *Library Public Relations, Promotion and Communications*

chapter objectives

1. Assess the use of various promotional techniques to promote library services, including public relations activities.
2. Discuss setting promotional goals and objectives.
3. Discuss the development of promotional strategies and tactics.

The Alliance Library System (ALS), a consortium of 286 member libraries (rural and urban public libraries, state university and private college libraries, corporate libraries, and public school libraries) in central and western Illinois, was asked to "help articulate the value of its libraries to their constituents," said Karen Stott Bersche, communications and partnerships consultant at ALS. She quoted Valerie J. Wilford, ALS executive director, as saying, "We knew our members had many different needs. How could we design a publicity campaign suitable for all of them? We needed to define our focus." Wilford took the textbook approach to the project: Research first, campaign next.

Research partner Illinois Institute for Rural Affairs asked almost 3,000 library customers what they thought their libraries should be doing. The "winner" of the survey was interlibrary loan, the service most valued by customers in both rural and urban areas. ALS now had a focus for a public awareness campaign, which would generate goals, objectives, strategies, and tactics. The goal was to let the public know that each of the 286 member libraries could provide registered borrowers with access to millions of books, access to library catalogs across Illinois, and access to full-text databases and reference materials not available on the Internet. The focus was endorsed by their Alliance Advisory Council, which appointed a public relations planning team and hired First Communications, a Chicago public relations firm.

According to Bersche, some advisory council members "wanted a campaign that's as popular and successful as the Chicago cows" (a public art project that took Chicago by storm in 1999). There was a round of laughter and comments about animals native to central Illinois—plus comments about the millions in tourism dollars the cows had generated in Chicago the previous summer. The public relations planners took the notion to heart, and that's how the PIGS (Partners in a Great System: Library Advocacy through Partnerships) campaign was born. The objective was to have more than 100 PIGS given themes, decorated by local artists and displayed in member libraries of all types. The team took out full-page ads in the four major newspapers, developed a map of all PIGS locations in a 14,000-square-mile service region, identified potential corporate sponsors, and acted as "PIGS Central" to assure that there were no duplicate PIGS names. Harry Porker was the first name to go, followed by (among many others) Hams Christian Andersen, Hammy Sosa, Ham Sawyer, Oinkelberry Finn, and Pigg E. Banker (life-sized fiberglass pigs sold for $225). ALS and its logical corporate partner—the Illinois Pork Producers Association—held a joint kickoff press conference. Media kits and a website with downloadable promotional material, which member libraries could customize, were developed; local sponsors came forth; and local and regional news coverage was generated.

By the end of the yearlong campaign, there were 250 PIGS at member libraries or sponsor's sites. Throughout the area, when somebody asked a library staff member why there was a pig in the library, the staffer started a conversation about ALS and the interlibrary loan system that made so many items available to local library customers. Bersche quotes Director Wilford as saying, "It would have cost more than $110,000 to buy the newspaper coverage generated by the PIGS campaign."[1]

The ALS assessed the needs of their member libraries. They scanned their environment to assess what was going on within the communities of their member libraries and around the state, which provided information about public perception of library services and the popular and successful Chicago cows campaign. ALS set a goal to make the public aware of their interlibrary loan service, and they established a planning team. The team set objectives and worked with a Chicago public relations firm to develop and implement strategies and tactics for the campaign. The goal of public awareness was accomplished and the objective of having 100 PIGS displayed in member libraries and partner sites was surpassed.

MARKETING AND PUBLIC RELATIONS

Some people would define the ALS campaign as a marketing campaign; others would call it a public relations campaign. Pure marketers consider public relations to be a subset of marketing, whereas many public relations practitioners consider it to be a distinct discipline. Both are definitely related under the promotion umbrella. Promotion covers all the ways you communicate. It includes the broad categories of sales, advertising, public relations, and a long list of specific techniques from brochures to the annual holiday open houses to public service announcements on the radio. Figure 8-1 lists and describes components of marketing and public relations. As you can see, both marketing and public relations are much more than promotion. Promotional techniques are, however, the most visible activities of both.

FIGURE 8-1
Marketing and Public Relations Basics

Marketing	Public Relations
Get to know your customers	Get to know your community
• Market research	• Opinion research
Segment and target your market	Segment and target your market
• What unmet needs will you develop products and services to meet? (library service response choices)	• What opinions will you influence? (create, reinforce, or dispel)
Develop strategies for the marketing 4 Ps	Develop strategies for communications programs
• Broad, long-range goals	• Broad, long-range goals
• Specific short-range objectives that are measurable	• Specific short-range objectives that are measurable
Marketing 4 Ps	Communications programs
• *Product:* Materials, programs/services, something of value	• *Publicity:* News releases, press conferences, newsletters
• *Price* (to a library customer): Cost in time, convenience, ease of use, and money	• *Advocacy:* People with favorable opinions about your organization influence others
• *Place:* Location and persons from which you can obtain the product	• *Special events:* Arrange for events to highlight positive attributes of your organization
• *Promotion:* "Paid" techniques that motivate people to use/buy products/services	• *Product promotion:* "Free" techniques that motivate people to use/buy products/services
Evaluate, Evaluate, Evaluate	Evaluate, Evaluate, Evaluate

Source: Pat Fisher, "Marketing and Public Relations Basics," presentation to American Library Association, ALTA Preconference, New Orleans, LA, June 23, 1999.

PROMOTING YOUR LIBRARY

It is important not to miss any opportunity to promote your library, its good work, and its contributions. It is best to decide, as you write the controls to implement your marketing effort, which promotional tools and techniques are likely to give the desired return on investment (ROI). Of course, midcourse adjustments may become necessary.

Generally speaking, promotion is designed to cause people, library users or non-users, to act. Knowing the messages you want to give to whom and for what purpose is the first step in developing your marketing communications and public relations plan. Once this is determined, your promotional techniques can be defined.

Knowing the attributes of your service can often lead to selecting a particular set of promotional techniques. For example, if your library upgrades its website, you might consider television and radio public service announcements. Print advertisements, internal newsletter announcements, banner ads (on websites), and customized bookmarks are also ways to promote awareness and increased use of the improved website.

The importance of the budget cannot be overemphasized. Many promotional campaigns go into cost overrun. Worse yet, for many campaigns the ROI is not positive. It is crucial, then, to delineate a promotion plan clearly, with the marketing and public relations techniques and their associated costs identified.

MARKETING TOOLS AND TECHNIQUES

Promotional techniques associated with marketing activities usually require a financial outlay or pro bono donation from a sponsor or partner. An outlay is an expense item that should be reflected in the marketing budget. A selective list and short descriptions of the most commonly used techniques follow:

Advertising. Advertising includes such activities as display ads in magazines and newspapers, preprinted inserts and circulars in magazines and newspapers, billboards, and paid radio, cable, and TV spots. Flyers and hand-painted signs (e.g., "Circus Coming to Town") posted to announce an event or new service are also considered advertising, though they are not always as effective as paid advertising in commercial venues.

Brochures. Brochures are printed publications that describe a service or the library in general. They normally both give a description and tell about means of access. They often include photographs or other graphics.

Celebrity Endorsements. Having news reporters, sports figures, or other celebrities endorse your library or a particular service is an excellent tool for building rapport with target markets. This is a popular approach: witness the library READ posters.

Contests. Anything from read-a-thons to contests that involve guessing how many jelly beans are in a jar on your circulation desk can generate interest in the library and its services.

Direct Mail. Direct mail can be a good tool to reach new markets. To be effective, a direct mail campaign requires good target market intelligence. You want to pay only to reach the people who will most likely respond to your message. The direct mail piece should have graphics and a message that appeals to your target market. Sending out a generic piece that blankets the community is sure to generate a low response rate.

Exhibits. Setting up exhibits in the library or at community fairs or other community venues is a good way to highlight the library or a service. Allowing community members to set up displays in the library is also effective; it is a good draw to the library, and the exhibits are conversation starters.

Open Houses. Food, fun, and fellowship draw both users and non-users. Hold a yearly open house and use it as a time to announce new services, or hold a special open house to announce or launch a new service.

Posters. Many people like reading and receiving posters. A poster that contains appealing graphics and your logo or brand of the service you want to promote is often well received. In creating posters, consider what might appeal to your target market and where you may be able to place the posters.

Telemarketing. Telemarketing involves people making telephone calls to a list of current customers or potential customers to give them a prepared message. The person making the call is given a script to follow. Telemarketing is usually used as part of a direct mail campaign. It is the call that is made to reinforce the direct mail piece and obtain the action (money, commitment, etc.) desired by the campaign. If you have to pay people to make the calls, this can be an expensive part of the campaign. Libraries engaged in fund-raising (development) sometimes have members of friends groups or their foundations make the telemarketing calls.

Trade Fairs. Increasingly, many organizations in the community and on college campuses are organizing festivals at which they solicit businesses and other organizations to participate by setting up booths. Academic and public libraries should participate; these are good places to promote the library and its services as well as develop partners.

Videos. If a picture is worth a thousand words, moving pictures must be worth a billion. Makers of luxury cars send prospective customers videos along with their slick brochures. They want prospects to get an up-close look at the features of the car and possibly begin to imagine themselves behind the wheel. Libraries could videotape story hours and other programs presented in the library. The videos could be put in the circulating collection. Customers who view the videos may imagine themselves taking advantage of the library's services in the future.

PUBLIC RELATIONS TOOLS AND TECHNIQUES

Promotional techniques associated with public relations are normally activities that do not require a financial outlay. They do, however, require staff time and in many cases the expertise of a public relations firm, which is an expense. Often there is also an expense in creating video and radio content used in public service announcements. Most large-scale public awareness campaigns also employ the use of specialty advertising items such as bags, bookmarks, mugs, pens and pencils, and T-shirts. Anticipated expense items should be reflected in your marketing budget. A selected list and short descriptions of the most commonly used techniques follow:

Anniversary Celebrations. The first anniversary of something and its subsequent five-year anniversaries are always great occasions to have an open house or other special event or give away specialty advertising items (pens, pencils, mugs).

Annual Reports. Annual reports may be elaborate or simple; they provide an excellent opportunity to promote selected services and to solicit resources.

News. Editorials, letters to the editor, opinion editorials (op-ed pieces), feature stories, news conferences, and press releases are all forms of publicity or an attempt to use news as promotion. This is the least controllable of all the promotional techniques. Given that negative publicity is easier to get than good publicity, you must make a concerted effort to build good relationships with the news media in your community. Identify the right people at the various media outlets to keep informed about what is happening at your library. Be sure to send well-crafted press releases to invite coverage of an event or to announce a service. A press release should answer the questions Who? What? Where? When? and How? It should be organized like an inverted pyramid, with the most important information at the top. In addition to sending press releases, pitch story ideas to your contacts and make news by arranging to have a newsmaker (important official, sports star) headline a news conference to announce an event or new service. Get library supporters to write letters to the editor or op-ed pieces about the good things your library is doing.

Newsletters. Newsletters can be distributed on an annual, semiannual, quarterly, or (if you have the resources) monthly basis. Newsletters provide an opportunity to write stories about what is happening at the library. Various services and customers can be spotlighted. A calendar of events can be provided. Newsletters can be displayed at the circulation or information desks or in the retail establishments of various businesses. On occasion, they could be mailed to library supporters.

Public Service Announcements. Public service announcements, often called PSAs, may be 30, 45, 60, or 90 seconds long. They are broadcast from radio, basic television, or cable television stations. Stations usually have a preferred format. Many radio spots just require you to send a script to be read by their radio personality. As a rule of thumb, allow 2.5 seconds for every word; thus, a 30-second spot is long enough for about seventy-five words. Television spots must be recorded in a studio. Sometimes you can get the station or a recording studio to donate the resources to write the script and produce the announcement.

Public Speaking. Having library staff, trustees, and members of friends groups volunteer to speak to civic or community groups, schools, or special interest groups is an excellent way to generate goodwill and support.

Signage. Effective signs and clear directions to your library and within your library can give people a positive experience with your library rather than a frustrating experience.

Talk Shows. Cable TV and radio stations have an obligation to provide community service programming. Many stations invite nonprofit organizations to their talk shows to highlight the organization's services. Libraries should take every opportunity to place staff, trustees, or volunteers on these shows.

TOOLS AND TECHNIQUES COMMON TO MARKETING AND PUBLIC RELATIONS

Some tools and techniques, which may or may not have a price tag, are shared by marketing and public relations. A selected list and short descriptions follow:

Networking. Library staff, trustees, members of friends groups, volunteers, and other library supporters all belong to personal networks. Keep these people informed of what is happening in your library; they can be great ambassadors for your library.

Special Events. Auctions, galas, "nights in the stacks," races, and the like are all opportunities to galvanize volunteers and staff to plan big events that get your library noticed. They are an opportunity to bring members of the community to a venue where you highlight library services. Often these events are planned as part of a library foundation's fund-raising activities, but they raise friends as well as funds.

Specialty Advertising. Specialty advertising items (mugs, magnets, pens, T-shirts, bookmarks), also known as "trinkets and trash" or tchotchkes, are a favorite technique of nonprofit organizations and businesses for building their brands. In most cases, the items are given to customers and prospective customers. The intent is to have the recipient use the item and remember the organization or business when they need a service the organization or business provides. Occasionally the items are sold to customers. Either way, having such items in the recipients' possession can serve to continue the branding of a service.

Websites. Library websites should be designed to provide information about the library's services in an appealing way. The site should be easy to navigate, and the information should be kept current. Websites can convey not only information but the library's culture and image—through graphic presentation and overall accuracy and currency of information provided.

Word of Mouth. Word of mouth is the most powerful form of advertising and public relations. Customers who like what you provide can become raving fans. They tell people they come in contact with about your services. Unfortunately, dissatisfied customers tell *everyone* they come in contact with about their bad experiences. It is the library's job to make sure customers have something positive to say.

ASSESSING PROMOTIONAL TECHNIQUES

To evaluate your promotion efforts, make a list of promotional techniques you have used and assess the effectiveness of each. Many marketing experts say you should consider these points in your critique:

Has this promotional tool produced good results?

Does it convey the image we want?

Does it address the right audience and speak to their particular values and needs?

From the list of promotional techniques described in this chapter, select those you have used in the past and evaluate their effectiveness on worksheet 11, the Promotion Audit. Make note of the techniques you should consider in developing the promotional campaign—those that will best implement strategies to achieve your marketing plan's objectives and goals.

PROMOTIONAL CAMPAIGNS, STRATEGIES, AND TACTICS

To develop your promotional strategies, review your description of the target market and your Promotional Audit (worksheet 11). Your promotional strategy may call for a small-scale, in-house promotional campaign with minimal, if any, outside graphic design or professional writing support. Or your strategy may call for a large-scale campaign requiring graphic designers, writers, or other communications professionals such as public relations firms.

Marcy Pride chaired the steering committee of a large-scale promotional campaign, Maryland Public Libraries' It's Never Too Early (see chapter 7). One of the initial strategies developed by the committee was to use Library Services Technology Act monies to develop promotional materials that could be used by all the libraries in the state. Additionally, the committee employed communications strategies that involved the Internet (website) and public service announcements (radio and television). To execute the tactics required to implement the strategies, they hired a public relations firm and set an initial campaign budget of $147,000.

Promotional Campaigns

If a large-scale promotional campaign is one of your strategies, you should issue a request for proposal (commonly known as an RFP) to several public relations firms. An RFP describes the service, target market, goals, and objectives. Let the firms suggest strategies and promotional techniques, along with the required budget, needed to implement your strategies and accomplish your goals and objectives. After you select a firm, provide these professionals with your positioning statement and completed worksheets to help them craft the message, appearance, and techniques of your promotional campaign.

If you are developing a small-scale promotional campaign, use your completed worksheets to determine what promotional techniques are the most effective with your target market. Word of mouth, for example, is an effective technique with teenagers. Once you decide on the techniques to be used in your promotional campaign, develop strategies and tactics to use these techniques. Also determine how much money you have to work with for a promotional campaign.

Promotional Strategies

Continuing with our chat reference example, the following promotional strategies could be employed to accomplish the goal of increasing teenage use of the library's website and the objectives for trials and a 10 percent increase in usage:

Encourage word-of-mouth advertising for the service. Buy "cool" trinkets that are popular with teenagers and can be imprinted with the chat reference logo. Give them away to students who use the service, complete a short survey, and then get a friend to use the service.

Submit a feature story idea about chat reference, complete with tips on getting the best results, to the high school newspapers in your target area.

Place posters in the library with the chat reference service logo showing happy teenagers using the service.

Each of these strategies will require specific tactics—tasks—to carry them out. Worksheet 4, section VII, Marketing Tactics / Action Plan, allows you to list your promotional tactics and techniques and estimate costs. Development of promotional tactics and other marketing mix tactics and budgeting are discussed in chapter 9.

---

quick-start tips

1. Select promotional techniques that will best highlight the service you want to promote and fit within your budget.

2. Use focus groups or interviews to test your target group's response to your graphics, design, and handouts prior to the final selection.

3. Use a lot of white space in your design of materials and website; be brief and avoid jargon.

4. Take full advantage of free tools and services.

5. Track outputs and outcomes as you go.

NOTE

1. Karen Stott Bersche, "Library System Rides a Pig to a Resounding PR Success," *American Libraries* 32 (September 2001): 44–47.

nine

Implementing Your Strategies
Developing Tactics, Budget, and Controls

Sooner or later all thinking and planning has to degenerate into work.

—Peter Drucker

chapter objectives

1. Define tactics and their relationship to strategy.

2. Discuss methods of setting marketing budgets.

3. Give examples of how to manipulate the controllable variables (tactics) to implement strategies.

4. Explain how controls are established to stay on schedule and within budget.

5. Give tips for a smooth implementation.

One of the goals of the American University Library was to improve efficiency. Access services librarian Helen Goldstein strongly believed that introducing a self–check out process as a new service would help accomplish this goal. But what strategies and tactics would attract a critical mass of potential library users willing to try self–check out?

A group of library faculty and staff formed a planning team to brainstorm strategies and tactics. One of the tactics was to enter a marketing contest, with a $5,000 prize, sponsored by 3M. The contest rules required that 100 or more library users participate in a launch-day activity to be eligible for the prize.

The team knew that finding 100 college students to participate in a library activity might not be easy. They agreed on the message they wanted to deliver: "Save time any time with the 3M Self–Check Out Time Machine." And who better to encourage this than noteworthy historical and literary figures, including Thomas Jefferson, Frederick Douglass, Jackie Onassis, Angela Davis, Clara Barton, Louisa May Alcott, and Frida Kahlo, just to name a few. All would arrive by the use of a seven-foot chrome and papier-mâché "time machine" in the library's lobby. They also decided to give prizes to students who used the self–check out service. Team members approached campus vendors for prize donations—these included savings bonds, phone cards, travel guides, and fax cards. By far the most impressive prize was an end-of-semester pizza party to be awarded to the dorm with the most students in attendance at the event.

Next, for tactics to get the word out, team members used all available communications channels—the campuswide newsletter, the student newsletter, flyers on campus bulletin boards, and an announcement on the university's voice-mail telecommunications bulletin board.

On launch day, crinolines rustled, capes flapped in the wind, swords clanged; literary and historical figures were everywhere. Everyone wondered—Was it a costume ball, or did we actually step a long way back in time? No, it was the twenty-first century at the circulation desk in the library on the campus of the American University in Washington, D.C. The library faculty, staff, and students were deliriously happy about the turnout and the air of excitement and expectancy surrounding the promotion and launch of "Check-It-Out Yourself," their new self-serve check out machine.

As each prizewinner was selected, library staff rang a bell and applauded. Students and library staff alike—nearly 300 of them by the end of the day—checked out books using the new self–check out machine. Nearly five times the usual number of items were checked out.

The major cost to this event, which won the library a $5,000 prize from 3M, was time. The team's successful appeal to vendors covered most of the other expenses and generated untold, invaluable goodwill with the American University campus community.[1]

The marketing planning team at American University put their plans to work successfully. They used a pioneering strategy of introducing the new service by educating their prospective customers. Their service tactics were service demonstrations and trial usage rewarded with prizes. Their place tactics included training staff to educate and assist customers and creating the appropriate atmosphere to introduce the new service. The promotional tactics included the use of newsletters, bulletin board flyers, voice-mail announcements, contests, word of mouth, and the launch-day special event. They implemented their strategies and tactics with a minimal budget. In fact, when you take into account the $5,000 prize, they could have a surplus in their marketing budget—to be used to implement additional strategies for other goals and objectives.

Are you thinking that, since you don't have much of a marketing budget, you should just list a few tactics to implement your strategies? The answer is no. This is the time to list all tactics that might be effective to accomplish goals, objectives, and strategies. You can pare down the list to fit the amount of money you have: you may be able to get grant funds; you may find ways to have some of the work done pro-bono; and you may find businesses or people willing to underwrite your expenses because you have such a detailed marketing plan.

DEVELOPING MARKETING TACTICS

Tactics tell you how to implement your strategy. Your tactics describe what is to be done to the variables you can control, when it will be done, and who will do it. The controllable variables are the "4 Ps" of marketing. The tactics you employ for each P has a price tag. Therefore, before you develop tactics for implementation, you need to think about how to establish a marketing budget.

Use worksheet 4, section VII, to list the tactics required to implement your strategies and to help determine the budget for your marketing expenditures. Given tight library budgets, you probably cannot do everything in the way of promotion you would like to. Make your choices based on what you believe will best help you meet your goals and objectives. If your choices include distribution of printed materials and press releases, consult the many books available on designing printed materials and books on public relations for help in writing press releases.

Determining Marketing Budgets

There are several ways to decide on the optimal level of marketing expenditures, as follows:[2]

Percentage Method. Some businesses base their marketing budgets on percentage of sales. For example, they set aside for marketing expenditures a given percentage (5 or 10 percent) of what they expect in revenues from sales for that year. Libraries don't have sales revenue but they do have a projected operating budget. Using a similar approach, libraries could opt to set aside, for example, 1 or 2 percent of their operating budget for marketing expenditures. This approach has the advantage of establishing a predictable budget each year.

Affordable Method. Many organizations, particularly nonprofit organizations, set the marketing budget on the basis of what they think they can afford. A manager assesses all competing claims for funds and arrives at an arbitrary residual amount that can be used for marketing expenditures. Many libraries tend to use this approach, if they consider spending money for marketing at all; too many librarians believe marketing is simply the supposedly free publicity they get from issuing press releases—feature stories in the newspaper and the occasional public service announcement on radio or television. This approach leads to inconsistent levels of funds for marketing each year.

Competitive-Based Method. Some businesses set their marketing budgets on their competitor's outlay for marketing. They investigate what their main competitors spend on marketing and set their budgets to match the outlay or to outspend the competitor. This approach is not practical for libraries, for a variety of reasons.

Objective-and-Task Method. Organizations that use the objective-and-task method develop their budgets by (1) defining their marketing objectives and strategies as specifically as possible, (2) determining the tactics that must be performed to achieve these objectives, and (3) estimating the costs of performing these tactics. The sum of these costs is the proposed marketing budget. This approach is good for libraries. Worksheet 4, section VII, accommodates this approach. You can list all the tactics needed to implement your strategies for each of the elements in the marketing mix, and you can estimate the costs. It is best to list the ideal set of tactics. If, after adding up the costs, you cannot afford to implement all the tactics, you can go back and pare down the list.

Tactics for Controllable Variables

Refer to the worksheets you have completed for each of your goals (worksheet 10), which contain objectives and strategies. Transfer the tactics needed to implement your strategies to worksheet 4, section VII, and assign responsibility for the tactics, dates, and budget.

SERVICE (PRODUCT) TACTICS

Three basic things can be done with any service. It can be introduced into the marketplace, it can be modified, or it can be withdrawn. Other actions also affect the implementation of a marketing strategy, including actions related to service quality, branding, and packaging.[3]

Your service strategies and tactics should be guided by your customers' needs and wants (chapter 5) and by what your customers think about the attributes of your service versus the service attributes of competitive alternatives (chapter 6). For example, a chat reference service for teenagers that was available only during the school day may need to be modified to be available 24/7, or at least late into the evening, to accommodate teenagers who often wait to the eleventh hour before working on homework assignments, even ones that require some research.

For the chat reference example used in previous chapters, possible service tactics for the strategy (chapter 7) of providing demonstrations to students and teachers are as follows:

What	Who	How Much
Investigate software vendors	librarian	#hrs/salary
Contract with software vendor	purchasing	vendor price
Have software for service operational	vendor	vendor price
Contract with Internet service provider (ISP)	purchasing	ISP price
Have Internet access operational	ISP	ISP price
Schedule and set up demonstrations	librarian	#hrs/salary

PLACE TACTICS

Place encompasses everything related to the location of the service, including the staff. In most cases, library services are available from the central library and all the branches. Some services are available only from the central library or specific branches, and others are available via the library's website. Determining the actions needed to facilitate your goals, objectives, and strategies regarding these outlets are place tactics.

In our chat reference example, the place the service is being offered is the library's website. Here are some possible place tactics for the strategy (chapter 7) of collaboration with other library systems and a reference vendor to provide 24/7 coverage:

What	Who	How Much
Investigate reference vendors	librarian	#hrs/salary
Contract with reference vendor	purchasing	vendor price
Propose the idea to librarians in other libraries	librarian	#hrs/salary
Negotiate letters of agreement with other libraries	librarian	#hrs/salary

And here are some possible place tactics for the strategy of developing an online interview script and training:

What	Who	How Much
Develop the online interview script	librarian	#hrs/salary
Schedule and set up training sessions	librarian	#hrs/salary
Conduct training sessions for librarians	librarian	#hrs/salary

PRICE TACTICS

Businesses sometimes use a low price tactic to introduce new services and other times use a price skimming tactic—setting a high price because there are no competitive alternatives. With the exception of some nominal fees, libraries do not charge a cash price for their services. Customers do, however, pay to use library services—in time and convenience. Strategies and tactics to discover perceived costs to customers and reduce them should always be examined. And don't forget the psychological aspects of price—customers relate price to perceived quality (chapter 6).

In our chat reference example, the price paid for the service may be inconvenience. Some price tactics for the strategy (chapter 7) of monitoring website access statistics are given below:

What	Who	How Much
Set up web access report capability	vendor	vendor price
Monitor web access reports	librarian	#hrs/salary

PROMOTIONAL TACTICS

Tactics for the promotional techniques discussed in chapter 8 are especially useful for introducing a new service or retaining customers in the face of high competition. Your main objective is to make the service known to the market and to present it in its most favorable light in comparison to the competitive alternatives. Keep in mind, though, that no organization has unlimited resources to spend on executing many tactics. Stay focused on what you are trying to accomplish.

In the chat reference example, the promotional strategies for the service are based on how the target market likes to communicate. Here are some possible promotional tactics for the strategy of encouraging word-of-mouth advertising:

What	Who	How Much
Order trinkets with imprint of service name	librarian	vendor price
Develop and mount survey on website	librarian	#hrs/salary
Record users who have been referred by friend	librarian	#hrs/salary
Mail trinkets to those making referrals	librarian	#hrs/salary/ postage

IMPLEMENTING THE MARKETING PLAN

You have been using worksheet 4, section VII, to help you determine all the tactics required to implement your strategies as well as a budget for your marketing expenditures. You can also use this section of worksheet 4 to set up controls to monitor the implementation of your marketing plan.

Successful implementation requires that you establish controls to monitor your progress on all your listed tactics. You want to stay on schedule, and you want to stay within budget. Describe the controls you set up to stay on schedule and within budget. Describing the controls reassures those that must approve your plan and supply the funds.

Establishing Controls

The first step in establishing controls is to assign responsibility for each tactic, or task. A specific person should take responsibility, not a work unit or group, because when everyone is responsible, no one is responsible.

ESTABLISHING START AND END DATES

Start and end dates should be established for each tactic. Set a firm date for accomplishing the goals set in the marketing plan, then work backward to set the dates for each tactic. For example, if the goals are to be accomplished by June 30 and this should take six months, then the first tactic must start on January 1. It is best to give a little padding in the dates to allow for slippage in accomplishing some tactics; if the first task will take ten days to accomplish, you might schedule the dates to have twelve days from start to end. Keep in mind that some tactics must be accomplished before others can start, whereas others can be done simultaneously, especially when there are different people responsible for each. Worksheet 4, section VII, allows you to name those responsible for each tactic and also to list start and stop dates.

MONITORING THE BUDGET

Monitoring expenditures as you implement the tactics of your marketing plan is also a critical control. Since you used worksheet 4 to estimate the budget for each tactic, you can compare it to your actual expenditures to see if you are staying within budget. On occasion you will go over budget for a specific tactic but come under budget for another tactic. If this over-and-under balancing act does not occur naturally, you may need to adjust your tactics and their price tags as you go along to stay within budget.

STAYING ON SCHEDULE

Section VII of worksheet 4 allows you to keep track of the status of each tactic. At monthly meetings, those responsible for implementing the marketing plan report on the status of their tactics. An *R* is placed in the status column if it is clear that some roadblock is preventing or will prevent the person responsible from completing the assigned tactic on time. This is a signal to the marketing committee chair and those higher in the chain of command to intervene to remove the roadblock and perhaps also adjust the dates of remaining tactics that depend on the completion of the tactic in jeopardy. A *Y* is placed in the status column when it appears that the tactic may run the risk of going into jeopardy. This is a caution signal. The person responsible for the tactic or the committee chair may be able to take action to head off a roadblock. A *G* is placed in the status column when the tactic is progressing on schedule. And a *C* is placed in the status column when the tactic is complete.

FIVE TIPS FOR A SMOOTH IMPLEMENTATION

1. *Have a clear chain of command.*[4] Take time to decide who has the responsibility and authority to make decisions. Sometimes a group consensus is necessary. Other times, waiting for a consensus needlessly holds things up. Define what will work best in your situation at the outset. It has been our experience that empowering the marketing committee chair to make decisions when it is not practical to involve the entire group keeps the project on schedule. It is also helpful to have someone or several people at the highest level of the organization—a project champion or a steering committee—for the marketing committee chair to consult with to clear roadblocks or to seek advice.

2. *Keep people updated.* People strongly affected by the plan should already be involved, but make sure everyone in the program or organization, as well as other key individuals, are aware of your marketing efforts. This creates additional support for the plan and often leads to unexpected ideas and helpful connections. We have found that making periodic presentations to groups of key individuals with a stake in the outcome of the marketing plan is a good way of keeping them updated. In addition, creating a website, with password protection, where draft documents and status reports can be mounted is also an excellent way of allowing people to control when they receive updates and how much information they want to review.

3. *Keep communication flowing among all those implementing the plan.* If more than one person is implementing the plan, make sure everyone on the team is updated on each other's progress. Changes in scheduling and timing need to be communicated all around.

Monthly meetings to report status and dissemination of the report (worksheet 4) are excellent ways to keep communication flowing.

4. *Be flexible and responsive.* Sometimes problems just aren't apparent until implementation is under way. If necessary, stop, regroup, and revise your plan. New ideas and opportunities also can pop up. Be open to expanded horizons.

5. *Evaluate and update regularly.* Be sure to evaluate progress toward your goals regularly. If things are working well, stay the course. If your situation changes, take time to update the plan.

quick-start tips

1. Convene a panel of subject matter experts to review the worksheets you have completed for each goal (worksheet 10) with your objectives and strategies. Also review the completed worksheets on your service, target market, competitive position, and marketing audit of the marketing mix elements.

2. Use worksheet 4 to list the tactics you plan to use to implement your strategies.

3. Empower the marketing committee chair to develop a preliminary worksheet that assigns responsibility for tactics, along with start and end dates. Then convene a meeting with everyone who will have responsibility for implementation to confirm the dates, making adjustments where necessary.

4. Have everyone involved with the implementation agree on dates for monthly meetings for the duration of the project

NOTES

1. Helen Goldstein, telephone interview, March 25, 2003.
2. This section adapted from P. Kotler and A. R. Andreasen, *Strategic Marketing for NonProfit Organizations* (Upper Saddle River, NJ: Prentice-Hall, 1996), 358–360.
3. See, for example, W. A. Cohen, *The Marketing Plan*, 2d ed. (New York: John Wiley, 1998), 61.
4. These five points adapted from G. J. Stern, *Marketing Workbook for Nonprofit Organizations* (St. Paul, MN: Amherst H. Wilder Foundation, 1990), 67.

ten

Closing Thoughts
Summaries and Evaluation

Evaluating is itself the most valuable treasure of all that we value. It is only through evaluation that value exists.

—Friedrich Wilhelm Nietzsche

1. Present the elements needed in the marketing plan summary.
2. Point out a few of the concepts we hope you have learned.
3. Discuss the need to evaluate your marketing efforts.

Marketing Plan Summary for Chat Reference (hypothetical example)

Chat reference service is to be introduced in one county in Maryland. It will be the only online source of helpful answers from librarians available in real time day or night. Chat reference is accessed via the library's home page. The service will cater to the nearly 50,000 teenagers in the county enrolled in grades 9–12. The librarians who staff the virtual reference desk, from our library and partner libraries, will be trained to use software that allows both student and librarian to share the same web page view. They will also be trained to conduct reference interviews with remote users, thus assuring consistent, personalized service. State-of-the-art software and high-speed telecommunications lines will ensure that students do not encounter connection times of more than three seconds. Demonstrations of chat reference will be given to students and teachers at the county's high schools the first year the service is introduced.

The total start-up costs will be $125,000. Grants will cover the start-up costs, and the incremental operating costs will be absorbed into the library's operating budget. The library expects to attract 5,000 chat reference users in its first year, 7,500 in its second year, and 10,000 in its third year. On average, each user asks two questions a year, so by its third year chat reference should be receiving 20,000 questions a year. Chat reference use by teenagers enabled the library to reach its goal of increasing teenage use of the library's website by 10 percent a year over the three-year planning horizon. Promotional expenses for the service amount to $25,000 for staff time to conduct demonstrations, give-away trinket rewards for word-of-mouth referrals, and posters to advertise the service.

Chat reference will succeed because of the following differential advantages:

It is the only online source of helpful answers from librarians available in real time day or night for teenagers in the county.

The influence of the strongest competitor, self-directed web search with a friend, will be mitigated when teachers recommend that students use the chat reference service.

The level of service provided by the librarians will turn users into "raving fans" who spread the word about the service to their friends.

The increased quality of homework assignments turned in by students who use the service will motivate teachers to continue recommending the service to their students.

SUMMARIZING THE MARKETING PLAN

The final section of your marketing plan, section IX, contains the summary. As illustrated in the hypothetical vignette above, a closing summary is not the same as the executive summary in the beginning of your plan. According to William A. Cohen:

In the summary, you discuss advantages, costs . . . and clearly state once again the differential advantage that your plan for this product or service offers the competition. The differential or competitive advantage is what you have that your competitors lack. Basically it states why your plan will succeed.[1]

If you are seeking approval or funds to implement your marketing plan, the "bottom-line" people will look at this section of your marketing plan first. If they get a sense that the plan will succeed from this summary, then they will go back and look at the details of your plan.

LESSONS LEARNED

We hope you have found the information in the preceding chapters helpful and that you are enthusiastic about developing and implementing a marketing plan for one of the services or service families your library offers.

You've seen numerous examples of various kinds of library entities and their marketing plan successes. You can borrow some of their ideas or create your own. You've seen that imagination, creativity, and resourcefulness are key components to successful marketing and promotion activities.

You've developed a framework for understanding user target segments, and you've used the worksheets to begin your own marketing planning process on selected services. You also have a sense of what kinds of promotional approaches to consider to generate awareness and to enhance user satisfaction. In addition, we hope that you've learned these lessons:

Marketing, like strategic planning, is a strategic management activity.

Collecting and analyzing data about the people in your service area and the environment in which your community exists is the first step in creating your marketing plan.

The single most important element of the marketing mix is the service you offer; it must be fundamentally attractive to some target market.

One of marketing's primary purposes is to develop customer relationships and allegiances to facilitate the process of exchanging something of value for something needed.

Every service and service provider has some form of competition.

Positioning is that desirable place in the customer's mind where he not only recognizes the service but can also recite its attributes.

The quality of customer service provided by your staff, the elimination of barriers to use the service, and the atmosphere and design of the place customers obtain your service are all part of marketing considerations.

Customers do pay a price to use your services; often it is paid indirectly in the form of tax dollars, tuition and fees, time, and convenience.

Promotion, which is designed to cause both library users and non-users to act, is the last step in the marketing mix.

Marketing *goals* (the endgame) are based on the strategic directions from your strategic plan; *objectives* are the means of quantifying your goals; *strategies* state the why and how of what you want to do; and *tactics* describe what is to be done, when it will be done, and who will do it.

Libraries should have a line item for marketing in their budgets.

Successful implementation of your marketing plan requires you to establish controls to monitor your progress.

EVALUATION IN A FEW WORDS

Planning, both strategic and marketing, is a cyclical activity. Plans that are made are executed. The strategies, tactics, and outcomes are monitored and evaluated. Lessons learned about the target market, the environment, and the marketing mix are fed back to be used in the next planning cycle. This cyclical activity is illustrated in figure 1-2.

As you implement your marketing plan, make it a practice to evaluate your actions as you go along, keeping track of both outputs and outcomes. Although some of us shy away from evaluation, in the long run it will be of great benefit to the library and its supporters and users to evaluate the processes and progress associated with all endeavors. To make it as painless as possible, we suggest answering a few simple questions:

What were we trying to accomplish?

In what time frame?

With what resources? To include money, staff, volunteers, etc.?

Did we meet our goals?

What went well?

What needs changing?

What lessons did we learn?

Of course, you may want or need to conduct a more elaborate evaluation. Or you may want to engage an independent group to do your evaluation. However you choose to evaluate the outcomes of your plan, it's important to include this piece.

CONCLUSION

Remember, a well-developed marketing plan

- helps you begin with the end in mind
- serves as a blueprint to reach the desired end, with each participant's contribution clearly delineated
- helps you determine how to secure and use resources
- helps you avoid problems and capitalize on opportunities

NOTE

1. W. A. Cohen, *The Marketing Plan*, 2d ed. (New York: John Wiley, 1998), 13.

MARKETING PLAN WORKSHEETS

This book contains eleven worksheets that are essential for implementing the marketing concepts described in this book. Readers are free to copy these forms for their use or to use the fillable PDF versions on ALA's website. Go to the ALA Store (www.alastore.ala.org) and click on the Web Extra tab on the lower left, or go directly to www.ala.org/editions/extras/Fisher09096.

1. Strategic Planning Self-Grade Card
2. Data Collection—Public Library
3. Data Collection—Academic Library
4. Marketing Plan Template
5. Service Life Cycle
6. Service Competitive Audit
7. Semantic Differential
8. Positioning Map
9. Place and Price Audit
10. Goal, Objectives, and Strategies
11. Promotion Audit

Strategic Planning Self-Grade Card

Grade your performance using the grading scale A–F. If you have more than four Fs and two Ds, you are not ready to develop a marketing plan. Look at figure 1-1, the Fix-It Tool Kit, for quick fixes to your strategic plan.

Phase	Key Questions	Grade (A–F)

Starting Up	1. How effective was our start-up process?
	    Did we develop a realistic timetable?
	    Did we set a realistic budget?
	    Did we lay out good ground rules for decision making and handling other tough topics?
		1.

	2. How effective was the facilitator or in-house staff?
	    Did we handle tough topics well?
	    Did we get the plan done on time?
		2.

Planning Process	1. How effective was our planning process? Did it help protect us or get us more resources?	1.

	2. How effective was the planning team?
	    Did it include a good mix of stakeholders, staff, administrators, board/faculty, and others?
	    Was the group representative of stakeholders such as businesses, youth, homeschool families, ethnic/racial groups, and community leaders/elected officials?
		2.

	3. How supportive was our dean or director?
	    Was he/she enthusiastic and willing to commit his/her own time?
	    Did he/she state that criticism was welcome, that no topics were taboo?
		3.

	4. How well did our planning model work?
	    PLA's *New Planning for Results*
	    Facilitator's own model
	    Our own model
		4.

	5. How well did we assess community trends and needs?
	    Obtained quantitative data
	    Obtained qualitative data
	    Got input from stakeholder groups, leaders
	    Reviewed all data and ideas carefully
		5.

	6. How effective were we in gathering different types of data?
	    Demographic data
	    Behavioral data (library usage data)
	    Psychographic data
	    Library resource data
		6.

(cont.)

Phase	Key Questions	Grade (A–F)

Plan's Contents	1. Does the plan contain all these elements?
	
	    Vision statement
	
	    Values
	
	    Mission statement
	
	    Goals and supporting objectives (also called outcomes and supporting strategies)
	
	    List of planning team members, affiliations
	
	    Description of methodology used
	
	    If methodology included *New Planning for Results,* does it have service responses for several of the thirteen areas?
	
	2. Does the companion action plan (business plan or annual work plan)
	
	    Link to specific goal/objectives?
	
	    Show steps to be taken?
	
	    List responsible persons?
	
	    Show target start and finish dates?
		1.
		
		2.

Status, Review, Update	1. How well have we planned steps to review and evaluate the plan and its implementation?
	
	    Do we provide written status reports for each goal/objective to the board at least semiannually?
	
	    Do administrators review the plan regularly?
	
	    Does the performance review of managers evaluate how well they have implemented appropriate steps in the plan?
	
	2. How well have we institutionalized the planning cycle?
	
	    Do administrators and managers gear up to update the plan every 3–5 years?
		1.
		
		2.

Implementation	1. How well have we integrated the plan into the operational and capital budgets?
	
	    Does every FY budget cite goals and objectives related to the plan?
	
	    Do departmental and managerial goals cite or support the plan?
	
	2. How well have we used the planning process and the plan's implementation progress to achieve a higher visibility for the library?
	
	    Have we received regular publicity on progress in achieving the plan?
	
	3. How well have we used the plan to help to
	
	    Develop and update marketing plans?
	
	    Create branding and positioning strategies?
	
	    Fight against cuts in standards and budgets?
	
	    Allocate resources such as staff, dollars, space?
	
	    Advocate for more resources?
	
	    Recruit staff and board members?
		1.
		
		2.
		
		3.

TOTAL: _____ A _____ B _____ C _____ D _____ F

COMMUNITY DATA

1. How many people live in your service area? _____

   (If your library serves significant numbers of people in neighboring communities, you may wish to keep two sets of population numbers here, one that includes only those within your legal service area and another that includes people in neighboring communities.)

   What is the percentage increase/decrease in 5 or 10 years? _____

   What is the projection for the next 5 years? _____

   What is the population trend (increasing, decreasing, same)? _____

   Source: _____

2. Of the people living in your community, what percentage are age

	5 years ago	*Now*	*In 5 years*
Under 5	_____	_____	_____
5–13	_____	_____	_____
14–18	_____	_____	_____
19–21	_____	_____	_____
22–65	_____	_____	_____

   (Feel free to change the above age ranges to fit the way your source reports numbers. Also, use numbers for cohorts such as Generation X or baby boomers if they are available. Knowing the percentage makeup of these cohorts may be useful in developing your marketing strategy.)

   What trends do you notice? _____

   Source: _____

3. What are the ZIP codes in your serving area? _____

   (Use the Claritas website, http://www.yawyl.claritas.com, to identify the five most prominent PRIZM NE segments for each ZIP code. Record the segment names and descriptions on a separate sheet. This information will be helpful if you decide to base your marketing strategy on lifestyle market segmentation.)

4. How many single-parent households are there?

   5 years ago _____   Now _____   Projected in 5 years _____

   What trends do you notice? _____

   Source: _____

5. What languages are spoken in the homes of the people in your community? _____

   _____

   What trends do you notice? _____

   Source: _____

6. What ethnic groups are represented in your community? _____

   _____

   What trends do you notice? _____

   Source: _____

(cont.)

99

7. What is the median family income in your community?

 5 years ago _____ Now _____ Projected in 5 years _____

 What trends do you notice? _____

 *Source:*_____

8. What percentage of the families in your community have incomes below the poverty line?

 5 years ago _____ Now _____ Projected in 5 years _____

 What trends do you notice? _____

 *Source:*_____

9. What percentage of your community is unemployed?

 5 years ago _____ Now _____ Projected in 5 years _____

 What trends do you notice? _____

 *Source:*_____

10. Does your community's population change widely during different seasons?

 Which seasons? _____ +/– how many people? _____

 *Source:*_____

11. Who are your community's three largest employers? What do they do? How many people do they employ? How is this likely to be different in 5 years?

 1st largest _____ Employs _____

 Make/Do _____

 In 5 years_____

 2nd largest _____ Employs _____

 Make/Do _____

 In 5 years_____

 3rd largest _____ Employs _____

 Make/Do _____

 In 5 years_____

 *Source:*_____

12. What are the major industries in your community (if different from major employers listed in 11)? What do they do? How many people do they employ? How is this likely to be different in 5 years?

 Name _____ Employs _____

 Make/Do _____

 In 5 years_____

 Name _____ Employs _____

 Make/Do _____

 In 5 years_____

Name _____ Employs _____

Make/Do _____

In 5 years_____

13. Where do people in your community get their information? Place a check mark by each source of information available locally. Indicate how many of each of the information sources are available.

How many?

_____ Local newspapers _____

_____ Local radio stations _____

_____ Local television stations _____

_____ Bookstores _____

_____ Video stores _____

_____ Music stores _____

_____ Local community access cable _____

_____ Internet service providers (ISPs) _____

_____ Other (community organizations, etc.) _____

*Source:*_____

Which of the above provide information in languages other than English? _____

_____

*Source:*_____

14. What other libraries are in your community? Place a check mark by each type of library in your community and indicate how many of that type of library there are.

How many?   *How many?*

_____ Elementary school _____   _____ College or university _____

_____ Junior high/middle school _____   _____ Hospital/medical _____

_____ High school _____   _____ Law _____

_____ Vocational technical _____   _____ Special _____

_____ Community college _____   _____ Other (name) _____ _____

*Source:*_____

15. How many public and private schools are in your community?
    List the number of each type of school.

Preschools _____ public _____ private

Elementary schools _____ public _____ private

Middle/junior high schools _____ public _____ private

Vocational/technical _____ public _____ private

Community colleges _____ public _____ private

Colleges/universities _____ public _____ private

*Source:*_____

(cont.)

16. Approximately how many homeschooling families are there in your community?

    5 years ago _____ Now _____ Projected in 5 years _____

    What trends do you notice? _____

    *Source:*_____

17. What percentage of the people in your community age 25 and older have at least a high school diploma or GED? (Note: This includes all technical school and college graduates.) What percentage have at least 2 years of college? What percentage have at least 4 years of college?

    Diploma/GED _____ 2 yrs college _____ 4 yrs college _____

    What trends do you notice? _____

    *Source:*_____

18. How many social service providers are located in your community?

    Nursing homes (extended care) _____

    Day-care centers _____

    Shelters/halfway houses/drug treatment centers _____

    Youth and recreation centers _____

    Other (list) _____

    What trends do you notice? _____

    *Source:*_____

19. List (for small library communities) or estimate (for larger communities) the number and types of the organizations in your community (service groups, clubs, etc.).

    _____

    _____

    _____

    What trends do you notice? _____

    *Source:*_____

LIBRARY USER DATA

20. How many people are registered cardholders in each age category?

	5 years ago	*Now*	*In 5 years*
Under 5	_____	_____	_____
5–13	_____	_____	_____
14–18	_____	_____	_____
19–21	_____	_____	_____
22–65	_____	_____	_____

(Feel free to change the above age ranges to fit the way your source reports numbers. Also, use numbers for cohorts such as Generation X or baby boomers if they are available. Knowing the percentage makeup of these cohorts may be useful in developing your marketing strategy.)

What trends do you notice? _____

*Source:*_____

21. Estimate the current number of regular users (usage greater than 4 times per year, or your definition of regular use), occasional users (usage less than 4 times per year), first-time users (card issue date less than 1 year old), and former users (cards have expired).

	Regular	*Occasional*	*First-time*	*Former*
Under 5	_____	_____	_____	_____
5–13	_____	_____	_____	_____
14–18	_____	_____	_____	_____
19–21	_____	_____	_____	_____
22–65	_____	_____	_____	_____

(Feel free to change the above age ranges to fit the way your source reports numbers. Also, use numbers for cohorts such as Generation X or baby boomers if they are available. Knowing the percentage makeup of these cohorts may be useful in developing your marketing strategy.)

What trends do you notice from 5 years ago?_____

*Source:*_____

22. What is the circulation per capita, and how many visits per capita were made, for each age group?

	Circulation	*Visits*
Under 5	_____	_____
5–13	_____	_____
14–18	_____	_____
19–21	_____	_____
22–65	_____	_____

(Feel free to change the above age ranges to fit the way your source reports numbers. Also, use numbers for cohorts such as Generation X or baby boomers if they are available. Knowing the percentage makeup of these cohorts may be useful in developing your marketing strategy.)

What trends do you notice from 5 years ago?_____

*Source:*_____

23. How many reference/information transactions occurred via the following modes?

In-library _____   By telephone _____   Online _____

What trends do you notice from 5 years ago?_____

*Source:*_____

24. What is the rate of electronic usage? How many times are resources accessed remotely? How many are resources used in-house?

Remote access (# hits) _____   In-house access _____

*Source:*_____

(cont.)

25. How many people attended programs?

    Children's _____   Young adult _____   Adult _____

    What trends do you notice from 5 years ago? _____

    Source: _____

26. What are the demographics of your heavy, medium, and light users?

	Age range	Gender	Ethnicity	Income level	Service used
Heavy	_____	_____	_____	_____	_____
	_____	_____	_____	_____	_____
	_____	_____	_____	_____	_____
Medium	_____	_____	_____	_____	_____
	_____	_____	_____	_____	_____
	_____	_____	_____	_____	_____
Light	_____	_____	_____	_____	_____
	_____	_____	_____	_____	_____
	_____	_____	_____	_____	_____

    What trends do you notice from 5 years ago? _____

    Source: _____

27. On what occasions do people use the library heavily? What are the demographics
    of the users on those occasions? (Examples: School-age children visit June–August
    for summer reading clubs; adults visit January–April for tax forms.)

Occasion	*Demographics (age/gender/ethnicity, etc.)*
_____	_____
_____	_____
_____	_____

    Continue on separate sheet.

    What trends do you notice from 5 years ago? _____

    Source: _____

    Completed by _____   Date completed _____

    Library _____

Source: Adapted from worksheets in Sandra Nelson, *The New Planning for Results* (Chicago:
American Library Association, 2001), 282–286, 291–295.

COMMUNITY DATA

1. How many students, undergraduate and graduate, are enrolled at your institution? _____

   What is the percentage increase/decrease in 5 or 10 years? _____

   What is the projection for the next 5 years? _____

   Source: _____

2. Of the total student body on your campus or distributed campuses, what percentage are

	5 years ago	*Now*	*In 5 years*
Freshman	_____	_____	_____
Sophomore	_____	_____	_____
Junior	_____	_____	_____
Senior	_____	_____	_____
Graduate	_____	_____	_____

   What trends do you notice? _____

   Source: _____

3. Of the total student body on your campus or distributed campuses, what percentage are

	5 years ago	*Now*	*In 5 years*
Full-time	_____	_____	_____
Part-time	_____	_____	_____

   What trends do you notice? _____

   Source: _____

4. Of the total student body on your campus or distributed campuses, what percentage

	5 years ago	*Now*	*In 5 years*
Live on campus	_____	_____	_____
Live off campus	_____	_____	_____
Are in distance ed program	_____	_____	_____
Are at a distributed campus	_____	_____	_____

   What trends do you notice? _____

   Source: _____

5. Identify the states where the majority of your undergraduate students come from.

   What are some of the ZIP codes in those states? _____

   _____

6. Identify the states where the majority of your graduate students come from.

   What are some of the ZIP codes in those states? _____

   _____

> (Use the Claritas website, http://www.yawyl.claritas.com, to identify the five most promi-
> nent PRIZM NE segments for each ZIP code. Record the segment names and descriptions
> on a separate sheet. This information may be helpful if you decide to base your marketing
> strategy on lifestyle market segmentation.)

(cont.)

105

7. What languages are spoken by the students on your campus or distributed campuses your library supports? _____

   What trends do you notice? _____

   *Source:*_____

8. What ethnic groups are represented on your campus or distributed campuses your library supports? _____

   What trends do you notice? _____

   *Source:*_____

9. What types of degree are granted on your campus or distributed campuses your library supports? Write in the major and indicate how many of that type of degree were granted in the past school year.

Major course of study	*Type of degree*			
	AA	BA/BS	Master's	PhD
_____	____	____	____	____
_____	____	____	____	____
_____	____	____	____	____
_____	____	____	____	____
_____	____	____	____	____
_____	____	____	____	____
_____	____	____	____	____
_____	____	____	____	____
_____	____	____	____	____

   Use additional sheets for additional courses of study.

   *Source:*_____

10. What types of degree can be pursued via distance education at your institution? Write in the major and indicate how many of that type of degree were granted in the past school year.

Major course of study	*Type of degree*			
	AA	BA/BS	Master's	PhD
_____	____	____	____	____
_____	____	____	____	____
_____	____	____	____	____
_____	____	____	____	____
_____	____	____	____	____
_____	____	____	____	____
_____	____	____	____	____
_____	____	____	____	____

   Use additional sheets for additional courses of study.

   *Source:*_____

11. Where do students on your campus get their information about campus or community events? Place a check mark by each source of information available locally. Indicate how many of each of the information sources are available.

		How many?
_____	Campus electronic discussion list	_____
_____	Campus newspaper	_____
_____	Local newspapers	_____
_____	Campus radio station	_____
_____	Local radio stations	_____
_____	Campus television station	_____
_____	Local television stations	_____
_____	Campus bookstore	_____
_____	Video stores	_____
_____	Music stores	_____
_____	Other (name) _____	_____

*Source:*_____

Which of the above provide information in languages other than English? _____

_____

*Source:*_____

12. What is the size of your faculty?

	5 years ago	*Now*	*In 5 years*
Assistant professor	_____	_____	_____
Associate professor	_____	_____	_____
Full professor	_____	_____	_____
Adjunct professor	_____	_____	_____
Department head	_____	_____	_____
Dean	_____	_____	_____
Other admin. faculty	_____	_____	_____
Total faculty	_____	_____	_____

What trends do you notice? _____

*Source:*_____

13. Identify ZIP codes of the faculty. _____

(Use the Claritas website, http://www.yawyl.claritas.com, to identify the five most prominent PRIZM NE segments for each ZIP code. Record the segment names and descriptions on a separate sheet. This information may be helpful if you decide to base your marketing strategy on lifestyle market segmentation.)

(cont.)

Data Collection—Academic Library (*cont.*)

14. What are the academic departments on your campus? Write in the department and indicate with a check mark the level at which courses are offered.

| | | *Type of degree* | | |
Academic department	AA	BA/BS	Master's	PhD
_____	___	___	___	___
_____	___	___	___	___
_____	___	___	___	___
_____	___	___	___	___
_____	___	___	___	___
_____	___	___	___	___
_____	___	___	___	___
_____	___	___	___	___

Use additional sheets for additional academic departments.

*Source:*_____

15. What are the major research interests of the faculty on your campus? (If your strategy calls for providing customized service, you may wish to gather this information for each faculty member by name.)

	Interest 1	*Interest 2*	*Interest 3*
Assistant professor	_____	_____	_____
Associate professor	_____	_____	_____
Full professor	_____	_____	_____
Adjunct professor	_____	_____	_____
Department head	_____	_____	_____
Dean	_____	_____	_____
Other admin. faculty	_____	_____	_____

*Source:*_____

16. How many research grants did faculty receive last year? In what discipline?

Grant discipline	*Number*	*Grant discipline*	*Number*
_____	___	_____	___
_____	___	_____	___
_____	___	_____	___
_____	___	_____	___
_____	___	_____	___
_____	___	_____	___
_____	___	_____	___
_____	___	_____	___

*Source:*_____

17. What organizations/companies are the three largest grant funding agencies? What do they do? How many people do they employ? How is this likely to be different in 5 years?

1st largest _____ Employs _____

Make/Do _____

In 5 years_____

2nd largest _____ Employs _____

Make/Do _____

In 5 years_____

3rd largest _____ Employs _____

Make/Do _____

In 5 years_____

*Source:*_____

18. How many articles or books were published by faculty last year? In what discipline?

Academic Department	*Number*	*Academic Department*	*Number*
_____	_____	_____	_____
_____	_____	_____	_____
_____	_____	_____	_____
_____	_____	_____	_____
_____	_____	_____	_____
_____	_____	_____	_____
_____	_____	_____	_____
_____	_____	_____	_____

*Source:*_____

19. Among the faculty and administrators, who are the library's biggest supporters? Who would you like to cultivate to become a bigger library supporter?

Current supporter	*Cultivate supporter*
_____	_____
_____	_____
_____	_____
_____	_____
_____	_____

Use additional sheets to list more names.

(cont.)

20. Where do members of the faculty get their information about campus or local community events? Place a check mark by each source of information available locally. Indicate how many of each of the information sources are available.

How many?

_____ Campus electronic discussion list   _____

_____ Campus newspaper   _____

_____ Local newspapers   _____

_____ Campus radio station   _____

_____ Local radio stations   _____

_____ Campus television station   _____

_____ Local television stations   _____

_____ Campus bookstore   _____

_____ Video stores   _____

_____ Music stores   _____

_____ Other (name) _____   _____

Source: _____

Which of the above provide information in languages other than English?

_____

*Source:*_____

LIBRARY USER DATA

21. Estimate how many of your library users are first-time users (new students, new faculty), regular users, occasional users.

	First-time	*Regular*	*Occasional*
Freshman	_____	_____	_____
Sophomore	_____	_____	_____
Junior	_____	_____	_____
Senior	_____	_____	_____
Graduate	_____	_____	_____
Faculty	_____	_____	_____

Have there been any trends over the 5 years? _____

_____

*Source:*_____

22. What are the numbers for circulation, library visits, and bibliographic instruction per capita?

	Circulation	*Visits*	*Bibliographic instruction*
Freshman	_____	_____	_____
Sophomore	_____	_____	_____
Junior	_____	_____	_____

Senior _____ _____ _____

Graduate _____ _____ _____

Faculty _____ _____ _____

What trends do you notice from 5 years ago? _____

Source: _____

23. How many reference/information transactions occurred by these modes?

In-library _____   By telephone _____   Online _____

What trends do you notice from 5 years ago? _____

Source: _____

24. What is the rate of electronic usage? How many times are resources accessed remotely? How many resources are used in-house?

Remote access (# hits) _____   In-house access _____

Source: _____

25. How many reserve requests did the faculty initiate 5 years ago? This year? What do you project for 5 years from now?

	5 years ago	*Now*	*In 5 years*
Assistant professor	_____	_____	_____
Associate professor	_____	_____	_____
Full professor	_____	_____	_____
Adjunct professor	_____	_____	_____
Department head	_____	_____	_____
Dean	_____	_____	_____
Other admin. faculty	_____	_____	_____
Total faculty	_____	_____	_____

What trends do you notice from 5 years ago? _____

Source: _____

26. What are the demographics of your heavy, medium, and light users?

	Undergraduate	*Graduate*	*Faculty*	*Service used*
Heavy	_____	_____	_____	_____
	_____	_____	_____	_____
	_____	_____	_____	_____
	_____	_____	_____	_____
Medium	_____	_____	_____	_____
	_____	_____	_____	_____
	_____	_____	_____	_____
	_____	_____	_____	_____

(cont.)

Light _____ _____ _____ _____

_____ _____ _____ _____

_____ _____ _____ _____

_____ _____ _____ _____

What trends do you notice from 5 years ago? _____

Source: _____

27. On what occasions do students and faculty use the library heavily?
    What are the demographics of the users on those occasions?

    Occasion   *Demographics (classification, faculty rank)*

    _____   _____

    _____   _____

    _____   _____

Continue on separate sheet.

What trends do you notice from 5 years ago? _____

Source: _____

Completed by _____   Date completed _____

Library _____

_____
Source: Modeled after public library worksheets in Sandra Nelson, *The New Planning for Results*
(Chicago: American Library Association, 2001), 282–286, 291–295.

Marketing Plan Template

Separate marketing plans should be developed for each product/service to be promoted or for each product/service family to be promoted. The marketing plan can be a few pages, with each section containing a couple of paragraphs, or each section can have a few pages.

TABLE OF CONTENTS

This section is recommended to ensure ease of review.

EXECUTIVE SUMMARY

This section presents a summary of the proposed plan for quick skimming by management.

SECTION I

Introduction *(See chapter 4.)*

Describe the existing or envisioned service in detail and explain how it fits into the market:

1. What are the benefits of the service?

   a. What is the core benefit being offered? (What is the customer really seeking? What need is the service really satisfying?)

   _____

   _____

   _____

   b. What benefits accrue to the community/campus when members of the target market use this service?

   _____

   _____

   _____

2. How are the characteristics of the service managed?

   a. What tangible item(s) does the customer see, feel, hear, touch, or receive as a result of receiving this service?

   _____

   _____

   _____

   b. What library personnel does the customer come in contact with to obtain this service? What technology does the staff person use to provide this service? How does the service function?

   _____

   _____

   _____

(cont.)

c. What steps are being taken to decrease the variability and ensure consistent quality when this service is delivered to the customer?

_____

_____

_____

d. What measures are being taken to balance supply and demand for the service?

_____

_____

_____

e. What do customers have to do or know to have the best "experience" in seeking the benefits of the service?

_____

_____

_____

3. What resources are needed to deliver the service?

a. What existing or additional hardware, software, electronic databases, print sources, etc., will be used or must be purchased to deliver the service? What staff reallocations or hiring is required?

_____

_____

_____

b. What partnerships with other organizations should be forged to supplement or complement capabilities? *(Identify areas to be complemented or supplemented here. Identify potential partners to target and strategies in Sections VI and VII, below.)*

_____

_____

_____

4. Where does the service fall in the service family hierarchy?

_____

_____

_____

5. What stage of the life cycle is the service in?

_____

_____

_____

6. What is the service description for your service?

_____

_____

_____

SECTION II

Target Market Description *(See chapter 5.)*

> *(Information about the characteristics of your target market may be obtained from a strategic plan or from other worksheets.)*

Basic Assumptions *(Record basic assumptions and/or indicate notations used to show that answers to questions 1–10 are assumptions, e.g., with *.)*

_____

_____

_____

1. What are the demographics of the target market?

   What is the size (how many people in total)? _____

   Age range: _____ Gender: Male _____ Female _____ Total _____

   Ethnicities: _____

   Languages spoken: _____

   Income range: _____

   Education level: _____

   Other(s): _____

   What are the significant demographic trends? _____

   _____

2. What are the geographic demographics that have marketing implications for your product/service?

   What is the area's population? _____

   What is the population growth pattern (stable, negative, positive)? _____

   How many public and private K–12 schools are in the community? _____

   What section of the country is the library and its target markets located (North, South, East, West)?_____

   What is the population density (urban, suburban, rural)? _____

   What type of media outlets are available (local, regional, national)? _____

   Other(s): _____

(cont.)

3. How do members of this target market use the library (behavioral data)?
   (Categories can overlap. Estimates could exceed 100% of total market size.)

   How many (or what percentage):

   Have library cards? _____

   Regularly use the library to borrow materials? _____

   Occasionally use the library to borrow materials? _____

   Formerly used the library to borrow materials? _____

   Would be first-time library users? _____

   Use materials in the library? _____

   Use reference services?

       In-library: _____

       Telephone: _____

       Online: _____

   Attend library programs?_____

   May have never used the library?_____

4. On what occasions (days of weeks, specific months, holidays) would members
   of this target market most likely use the service? _____
   _____
   _____

5. What are the significant library usage trends? _____
   _____
   _____

6. What are the five most prominent lifestyles within your target market (psychographics)?
   (Look up by ZIP code in "You Are Where You Live"—http://www.yawyl.claritas.com.)

   Lifestyle 1: _____

   Narrative description: _____
   _____
   _____

   Lifestyle 2: _____

   Narrative description: _____
   _____
   _____

   Lifestyle 3: _____

   Narrative description: _____
   _____
   _____

Lifestyle 4: _____

Narrative description: _____

_____

_____

Lifestyle 5: _____

Narrative description: _____

_____

_____

7. What are the significant lifestyle trends?

_____

_____

_____

8. What benefits of this service are valued most by members of this target market?
   What needs and wants are satisfied by the benefits of this service?

_____

_____

_____

9. Why is there a demand for this service in the target market? How much demand is anticipated?

_____

_____

_____

10. What are the media habits of the target market? What type (or specific outlet)
    of medium is viewed (e.g., conservative radio talk show; CNN on cable TV)?

Medium	*Hours/Week*	*Type (category)*
Television	_____	_____
Radio	_____	_____
Magazines	_____	_____
Newspapers	_____	_____

SECTION III

Current Market Situation (*See chapter 6.*)

1. Describe the competition. What alternatives can members of the target market obtain
   to satisfy their needs or wants? Or, what alternatives do members of the target have
   for spending their time?

Desire Alternative   *Assessment of competing alternative*

_____   _____

Generic Alternative   *Assessment of competing alternative*

_____   _____

(*cont.*)

Form Alternative

Assessment of competing alternative

_____

_____

Enterprise Alternative

Assessment of competing alternative

_____

_____

2. Describe the library's current position in the mind of members of your target market by answering one or more of the following questions:

   a. How do members of the target market currently perceive your library?

   _____

   _____

   _____

   b. What is your library's image compared to the image of a provider of a competing alternative?

   _____

   _____

   _____

   c. What is your library's image compared to the image of an ideal provider of a competing service?

   _____

   _____

   _____

   d. What is your current positioning statement for the service?

   _____

   _____

   _____

3. Describe the place (library's outlets) where the service can be obtained:
   (In narrative format, provide answers to applicable questions below.)

   a. How many physical outlets (main library, branches, bookmobiles, kiosks)?

   _____

   _____

   _____

   b. What are the dimensions of the physical outlets (square footage)?

   _____

   _____

   _____

   c. What are the virtual outlets (telephone, website)?

   _____

   _____

   _____

d. Are there barriers to use associated with your service?

_____

_____

_____

e. Describe the atmospherics of the physical or virtual outlet (look, feel of exterior and interior).

_____

_____

_____

f. How many librarians, support staff, and volunteers are available to deliver the service?

_____

_____

_____

g. What level of customer service do you provide?

_____

_____

_____

h. What special training has been given to staff to deliver the service?

_____

_____

_____

i. What customer service training has been given to staff?

_____

_____

_____

j. Will you need to forge partnerships to make this service available?

_____

_____

_____

4. What nonmonetary or monetary price does the customer have to pay to obtain your service? What is burdensome about obtaining your service?

   a. Time (waiting time, frustration)

   b. Convenience

   c. Transportation costs: public transportation, automobile costs, gas, parking

   d. Fees

   e. Other

(*cont.*)

5. What promotional techniques are being used for this product/service? How effective have the efforts been? *(See chapter 8 for a list of techniques.)*

Technique	Effective	Not effective	Not sure	Consider for promotional campaign	Comments

SECTION IV

Opportunity and Issue Analysis *(See chapter 6.)*

1. What are the main opportunities for the service? Why is it an opportunity?

Opportunity	*Why?*
_____	_____
_____	_____
_____	_____
_____	_____

2. How will you take advantage of each opportunity?

_____

_____

_____

3. What are the main issues facing this service? Why is it an issue?

Issue	*Why?*
_____	_____
_____	_____
_____	_____
_____	_____

4. What do you intend to do about each issue?

_____

_____

_____

_____

SECTION V

Marketing Goals and Objectives (See chapter 7.)

> *Marketing goals are derived from the strategic directions in your strategic plan that concern facilitating exchanges between your library and your customers. Goals set out the broad destination or "endgame" for the marketing strategy. Objectives turn the goals into specific quantifiable benchmarks for measuring progress.*

Some areas for goal and objective setting:

1. *Awareness*

   Goal: _____

   Objective(s): _____

   _____

2. *Usage*

   Goal: _____

   Objective(s): _____

   _____

3. *Staff knowledge and skills*

   Goal: _____

   Objective(s): _____

   _____

4. *Library funding*

   Goal: _____

   Objective(s): _____

   _____

(cont.)

5. Other: _____

   Goal: _____

   Objective(s): _____

   _____

6. Other: _____

   Goal: _____

   Objective(s): _____

   _____

SECTION VI

Marketing Strategies (*See chapter 7.*)

1. Core Marketing Strategy: _____

   _____

   _____

2. Positioning Strategy:

   a. What position, in the minds of your target market, will your library claim versus providers of competitive alternatives? _____

     _____

     _____

   b. Is there a dimension on which you can claim to be the best? _____

     _____

     _____

   c. Write your service's positioning statement. _____

     _____

     _____

3. Marketing Mix Strategies: How will the goals and objectives be accomplished?

   a. Service (Product) Strategies: _____

     _____

   b. Price: _____

     _____

   c. Place (can include partnerships): _____

     _____

   d. Partnerships: _____

     _____

   e. Promotion: _____

     _____

SECTION VII

Marketing Tactics / Action Plan (see chapter 9)

> This section states what will be done, who will do it, when it will be done, and how much it will cost. The chart can also be used to monitor the implementation (status) of these tactics (actions): R (for red) indicates not on schedule, could put other tasks in jeopardy; Y (yellow) indicates a possibility that the schedule will not be met; G (green) indicates that the action is on schedule; completed actions are indicated with C.

What	Who	When		Status	How much
		Start	*End*	*R/Y/G*	
Product					
Price					
Place					
Promotion					

How will budgets be established? Which strategy will you use? Explain.

1. Affordable method
2. Percentage of overall budget method
3. Competitive-parity method
4. Objective-and-task method

(cont.)

SECTION VIII

Implementation and Controls *(See chapter 9.)*

> This section states how the plan will be monitored. You may choose to incorporate the chart developed in Section VII into your plans.

SECTION IX

Summary *(See chapter 10.)*

> This section summarizes why the plan will succeed. Restate the advantages your plan for the product/service has over the competitive alternatives.

SECTION X

Appendixes

> This section includes all supporting information you consider relevant.

WORKSHEET 5
Service Life Cycle

Service _____

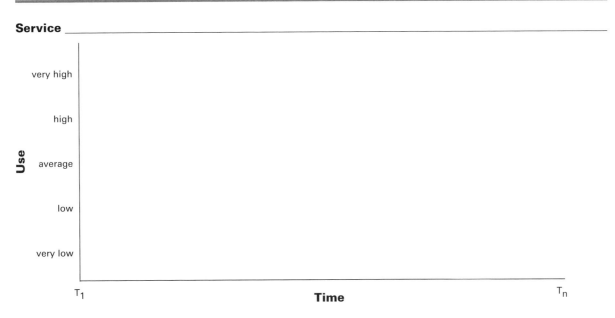

Sketch a rough draft of the volume of use curve of the type of service you want to introduce or promote based on information you have gathered about how the service has performed in the marketplace.

1. Gather information from library literature, library vendors, and your own records (if you have already introduced this service in your library) about the approximate volume of use for varying periods over the service's life so far. Remember: Think overall market. You don't need exact figures, only whether the use is very low, low, average, high, or very high.

2. Label the approximate time (T_1) when the service was first introduced.

3. Sketch the line showing volume of use starting at zero when it was introduced (T_1) and moving along the Time axis to T_2, T_3, T_4 . . . to the present (T_n).

    If this is a relatively new service, the line from T_1 to T_n may represent only a few years, and it may show volume of use going from zero to very low usage. For example, some public libraries have just begun to introduce e-book service, which allows customers to download books to computers or personal digital assis-

tants (PDAs). The e-books can be read for a period of three weeks or more before they expire and then can no longer be viewed on the computer or PDA. Library literature has discussed the technologies and copyright issues of e-books since the late 1990s. Recently, publishers and book jobbers have developed licensing agreements for libraries to offer the service. There should be ample sources of information on which you can base volume-of-use assumptions.

If this is a service that has been in the marketplace for some time, the line from T_1 to T_n may represent a few decades, and it may show volume of use going from zero until it plateaus and begins to decline in usage. For example, academic libraries have offered traditional reference service to students at the desk in the library for years. With the advent of Internet search engines, the volume of use of traditional reference service has declined. This phenomenon has been discussed in library literature, which should provide ample sources of information on which you can base volume-of-use assumptions.

4. Compare your sketch to figure 4-2 to determine the stage of the life cycle your service is in.

Source: Adapted from various product life cycle exercises in W. A. Cohen, *The Marketing Plan*, 2d ed. (New York: John Wiley, 1998).

Service Competitive Audit

List your competitors? How do you rank relative to the competition? Place a "+" to the left of the neutral point to indicate that your service is stronger. The farther left you place it indicates how much stronger it is. Place a "−" to the right of the neutral point to indicate that your service is weaker. The farther right you place it indicates how much weaker it is. List specific company or product names at the Enterprise level.

Desire Alternative	**Competing Alternative:** _____
1. _____	*Neutral* *Strong* ————————|———————— *Weak* ————————|———————— ————————|————————
2. _____	
3. _____	
Generic Alternative	**Competing Alternative:** _____
1. _____	*Neutral* *Strong* ————————|———————— *Weak* ————————|———————— ————————|————————
2. _____	
3. _____	
Form Alternative	**Competing Alternative:** _____
1. _____	*Neutral* *Strong* ————————|———————— *Weak* ————————|———————— ————————|————————
2. _____	
3. _____	
Enterprise Alternative	**Competing Alternative:** _____
1. _____	*Neutral* *Strong* ————————|———————— *Weak* ————————|———————— ————————|————————
2. _____	
3. _____	

Comments: _____

_____

✓ Goal, Objective, Strategy Checkpoint

How is your service's competitive strength at the Enterprise level?

☐ OK   ☐ Adjustment necessary*   ☐ Stress in promotion

* Develop goals, objectives, and strategies for adjustments.

WORKSHEET 7
Semantic Differential

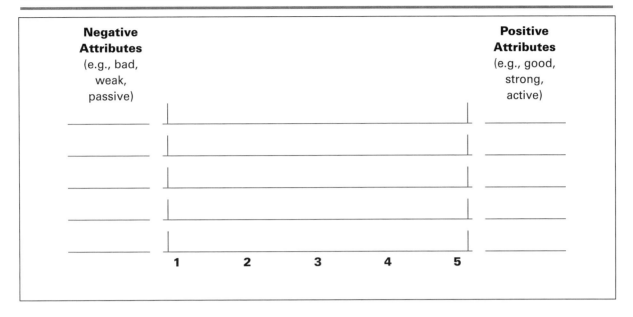

1. After determining the attributes people think about when they consider your service, construct a survey instrument. Use questions with evaluation, potency, or activity scales.

2. Ask respondents to rate one service from one organization at a time. If there are three competitive alternatives, you would have three sections for the respondents to complete, one at a time.

3. Total the results for each competitive alternative. Divide each total by the number of respondents to get the average.

4. Plot the average (line of means) for each alternative on one worksheet. (Use different colors or solid and dashed lines to distinguish the alternatives.)

5. Select one pair at a time to plot on a positioning map (see worksheet 8).

Positioning Map

Select the attributes—a pair at a time. Plot them on the *x* and *y* axes. For example, plot Easy/Hard and Fast/Slow on one map and User-Friendly/Not User-Friendly and Helpful Results/Unhelpful Results on another map.

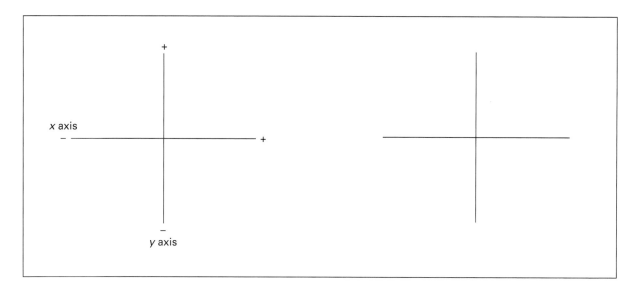

Draft your positioning statement. The positioning statement should make it easy for people to quickly grasp what your product or service is and what is unique about it.

✓ Goal, Objective, Strategy Checkpoint

Are you satisfied with your competitive position in the mind of your prospective customer?

☐ OK ☐ Adjustment necessary* ☐ Stress in promotion

* Develop goals, objectives, and strategies for adjustments.

Place and Price Audit

SECTION A

Place *(where the service is available)*

1. What type of outlet do you use to offer the service: a physical outlet (e.g., main library, branches, bookmobiles, kiosks, etc.) or a virtual outlet (telephone, website)? Describe the outlets (e.g., any of the following that apply: quantities, dimensions, transportation access, parking, neighborhood surroundings).

   _____
   _____
   _____

2. What are the "Plus" features about place (e.g., free parking, near a particular convenient spot)?

   _____
   _____
   _____

3. Are there any physical or emotional barriers to use (e.g., lack of equipment, poor signage, safety concerns)?

   _____
   _____
   _____

4. What are the atmospherics (e.g., outside look, inside functional and flow characteristics, "feel" of the inside, and materials that support the "feel")?

   _____
   _____
   _____

5. What type of customer service is offered? How do customers rate it? How is customer service quality sustained?

   _____
   _____
   _____

✓ Goal, Objective, Strategy Checkpoint

Are there any place issues to address (barriers to use, atmospherics, customer service)?

☐ OK ☐ Adjustment necessary* ☐ Stress in promotion

* Develop goals, objectives, and strategies for adjustments.

(cont.)

SECTION B

Price (*how customers pay to use the service*)

1. What nonmonetary or monetary price does the customer have to pay to obtain your service? What is burdensome about obtaining your service? What costs do customers perceive?

_____

_____

_____

✓ Goal, Objective, Strategy Checkpoint

Are there any price issues to address?

☐ OK   ☐ Adjustment necessary*   ☐ Stress in promotion

* Develop goals, objectives, and strategies for adjustments.

Goal, Objectives, and Strategies

Core Marketing Strategy (Differentiation, Cost Leadership, Focus): _____

_____

_____

Goal (one per page): _____

Time to Achieve: _____

Objective: *Time to Achieve:*

1. _____   _____

2. _____   _____

3. _____   _____

4. _____   _____

5. _____   _____

6. _____   _____

7. _____   _____

8. _____   _____

9. _____   _____

10. _____   _____

Strategy (choose from the market position or service life cycle strategies):

1. _____

2. _____

3. _____

4. _____

5. _____

6. _____

7. _____

8. _____

9. _____

10. _____

Promotion Audit

List the promotional techniques being used for this service. How effective have the efforts been? (See chapter 8 for a list of techniques.)

Technique	Effective	Not effective	Not sure	Consider for promotional campaign	Comments

List techniques that could be effective with some adjustments.

_____

_____

_____

_____

INDEX

Daviess County Public Library (Ky.), 7–8
decline stage strategies, 72
demographic data
    in combination with lifestyle data, 44
    definition, 14–15
    sources of, 14, 22
    and trend analysis, 18
differentiation core strategy, 67, 69
direct mail, 78
distribution innovation strategy, 71

E

e-mail reference life cycle stages, 39
evaluation, 81, 92–93
exhibits, 78

F

fees for services, 63
Flint Public Library (Mich.), 24
focus core strategy, 69
focus groups, 26, 82
follow the leader strategies, 71
fundraising and telemarketing, 79

G

Generation X, 18, 39
geographic expansion strategy, 70
Geographic Information System (GIS)
    software, 17
Goal, Objectives, and Strategies
    (Worksheet 10), 67, 74, 85, 131
goals and objectives
    collaborative services, 35
    and marketing audit, 65
    in marketing plan, 37
    quick-start tips, 74
    setting of, 66–74
    start and end dates, 87–88
    in strategic plan, 3, 9
Goshen College (Ind.), 5
growth stage strategies, 72

I

implementation
    marketing plan, 87–89
    strategic plan, 3, 4
increased usage strategy, 70
introductory stage strategies, 72

K

Kentucky Department of Libraries, 6
King County Library System (Wash.),
    56–57

L

Lakewood Public Library (Ohio), 11–12
library trustees, recruitment of, 6
life cycle curve, 37–39, 72
lifestyle analysis, 18–21
logos, 60

M

market challengers, 70–71
market followers, 71
market leaders, 60, 69–70
market niches, 71–72
market segmentation
    and awareness of services, 43–44
    definition, 44–45
    and inequality, 8–9, 45
    and trend analysis, 18
marketing
    tools and techniques, 78–79, 80–81
    vs. public relations, 76–77
marketing audit, 51–65
    quick-start tips, 65
    Service Competitive Audit
        (Worksheet 6), 55, 56, 126
marketing committee. *See* Subject matter
    expert panel
marketing mix, 24–25. *See also* Place;
    Price; Promotion; Service offers
    and customer service, 61
    in marketing strategy, 69, 73–74
Marketing Plan Template (Worksheet 4),
    113–124
    section I (Introduction), 39, 40–41
    section II (Target Market), 45,
        46–49
    section III (Current Market
        Situation), 60, 64
    section IV (Opportunity and Issue
        Analysis), 64
    section VII (Marketing Tactics), 82,
        84–85, 87–89
    section IX (Summary), 91
    and service strategies, 73
    use of, 27
marketing plans. *See also* Marketing Plan
    Template (Worksheet 4)
    contents of, 28
    existing product/service, 25–26
    implementation of, 87–89
    new products, 26
    quick-start tips, 29, 42, 89
    structure of, 26–28
    summary of, 91
marketing strategy, 65, 68–72
Maryland AskUsNow! service, 51
Maryland Public Libraries. "It's Never
    Too Early" Campaign, 26, 66, 81
mass marketing, 45
maturity stage strategies, 72
military planning, 25, 68–69
Millennial generation, 18
mission statement
    in collaborations, 35
    in strategic plan, 3, 9
Mississippi State University, 1

models for strategic plan, 3, 4
Morrison-Reeves Library (Ind.), 7–8

N

networking, 80
new market strategy, 70
new services, marketing of, 26
new users strategy, 70
new uses strategy, 70
news media, 79
newsletters, 79–80
niche market strategy, 70
non-users, identification of, 16

O

objective-and-task method of budgeting,
    85
objectives, 68. *See also* Goals and
    objectives
observation as data gathering, 23
occasion of use, 15, 16
open houses, 78
opportunity and issue analysis. *See*
    Marketing Plan Template
    (Worksheet 4): Section IV; SWOT
    analysis (Strengths, Weaknesses,
    Opportunities, Threats)
outreach, 6–9. *See also* Target markets

P

partnerships, 34–35
percentage method of budgeting, 85
perception variance, 59
perishable services, 33
pioneering strategy, 72
Place and Price Audit (Worksheet 9),
    129–130
    section A (place), 60, 73
    section B (price), 63–64, 73
place in marketing. *See also* Place and
    Price Audit (Worksheet 9)
    definition, 60–65
    strategies, 73
    tactics for, 85–86
planning committee, 42
planning process for strategic plan, 3, 4
positioning, 57–59. *See also* Branding
    in marketing strategy, 69–72
    and use of strategic plan, 6
positioning map, 59–60
Positioning Map (Worksheet 8), 59, 128
posters, 78
premiums. *See* Specialty advertising
pre-planning in marketing, 12–14
prestige goods strategy, 71
price, 63–64. *See also* Marketing Plan
    Template (Worksheet 4): Section
    III; Place and Price Audit
    (Worksheet 9)

psychological aspects, 62–63, 86
strategies, 73
tactics for, 86–87
PRIZM lifestyle segmentation system,
11–12, 18–21, 44
product life cycle. *See* Service life cycle
product/service offers. *See* Service offers
promotion, 75–82
in marketing mix, 24, 64
promotion plan, 77–78
quick-start tips, 82
strategies and tactics, 74, 81–82, 87
promotion audit, 81
Promotion Audit (Worksheet 11), 81,
132
promotional campaigns, 81–82
promotional items, 80
psychographic data, 18–21
public relations
tools and techniques, 79–81
vs. marketing, 76–77
public service announcements (PSAs),
80
public speaking as public relations, 80
Purdue University–Calumet (Ind.), 6

R

reference service life cycle, 39
repositioning, 72
research classes as service, 43
resources for services, 5, 17, 34–35
retentive strategy, 72
return on investment (ROI), 2–3
review and update of strategic plan, 3, 4
Richmond Public Library (B.C.,
Canada), 62

S

schedule for marketing plan, 88
self-check out process, 83–84
Semantic Differential Model, 57–59
Semantic Differential (Worksheet 7), 58,
127
Service Competitive Audit (Worksheet
6), 55, 56, 126
service description
development of, 39
and target markets, 50
service family hierarchy, 35–37
service innovation strategy, 71

service life cycle, 37–39, 72
Service Life Cycle (Worksheet 5),
39, 125
service mix, 36–37
service offers, 30–42
benefits, 31–32, 64
characteristics, 32–34
description of, 30
service (product) strategies, 73
service (product) tactics, 85–86
service proliferation strategy, 71
service providers to special populations,
outreach to, 7–8
service specialization, 72
service-feature specialization, 72
signage, 80
Silent generation, definition, 18
social marketing, 31–32
special events, 80
specialization for niche markets, 71
specialty advertising, 80
staff
care of, 61, 62
and customer relations, 33
and implementation, 88–89
stakeholders, communication with, 35,
88
standards and use of strategic plan, 5
start and end dates, 87–88
start-up phase of strategic plan, 2, 4
statistics. *See* Data collection
strategic directives, 68–69. *See also* Goals
and objectives
Strategic Planning Self-Grade Card
(Worksheet 1), 2–3, 97–98
strategic plans, 1–10
evaluation of, 2–3
fixes for, 4 (fig.)
implementation, 3, 4
and marketing planning, 6–9
quick-start tips, 9
and target markets, 50
use of, 5–6
strategy in marketing plan, 65, 68–72
subject matter expert panel
goals and objectives, 74, 89
marketing audit, 65
as marketing committee, 50
SWOT analysis (Strengths, Weaknesses,
Opportunities, Threats), 5–6, 64

T

tactics. *See also* Marketing strategy
development of, 84–87
responsibility for, 87, 88
talk shows, 80
tangible services, 32–33
target markets, 11–23, 43–50
and positioning, 57
quick-start tips, 50
response to promotional materials,
82
and review of service, 49
selection of, 45, 49
telemarketing, 78–79
timelines for marketing plans,
87–88
trade fairs, 79
trends, 12–14
behavioral data, 15–17
data collection, 17
demographics, 14–15
trend analysis, 17–22
uses of, 12–14

U

University of Florida, 24
University of Louisville, 43
University of Notre Dame, 5
University of Washington, 30–31,
56–57
usage rate, 16–17
user status, 15–16

V

values in strategic plan, 3, 9
variable services, 33
Veteran generation, definition, 18
videos, 79
vision statement
collaborative services, 35
strategic plan, 3, 9
volunteers, training of, 61

W

websites, 80
word of mouth, 80–81

Y

"You Are Where You Live" (YAWYL)
demographic data, 20

Patricia H. Fisher, BS Sociology, MAS, MLS candidate (2006), is an Independent Marketing and Public Relations Consultant. For fifteen years she was a Product Manager with Verizon Communications in the Consumer, Small Business, and Large Business units. Additionally, she has served libraries in a volunteer capacity for more than fifteen years: as member, Vice-president, and President of the Board of Library Trustees for Baltimore County Public Library; President of the Trustee Division of the Maryland Library Association; member, committee chair, First Vice-president, and President of the Association of Library Trustees and Advocates; and member of the Public Awareness Committee, the Committee on Legislation, and the Core Values Task Force of the American Library Association. She is currently enrolled in the College of Information Studies at the University of Maryland, College Park.

Marcy Pride, BA, MLS, MA, is Director of the library at Washington Bible College/ Capital Bible Seminary. Formerly she was a Public Library Consultant with the Maryland State Department of Education, Division of Library Development and Services. She has been a consultant to numerous nonprofit organizations including Big Brothers and Big Sisters, the Urban League, and the Association of Black Charities in the areas of public relations, organizational development, event planning, and partnerships. Additionally, she has been a reference librarian at Goucher College, American University, and the University of Maryland.

Ellen G. Miller, BS, MSLS, is President of the Ellen Miller Group of Lenexa, Kansas, a company specializing in positioning strategies for complex public and for-profit organizations. Prior to starting her own company, Ellen has worn all three library hats: staff member, friend, and trustee. She is founding president of the 900-member Kansas Library Trustee Association and a member of the Kansas State Library Advisory Commission and the Kansas Library Association's Legislative Committee. She is past Second Vice-president of the Association of Library Trustees and Advocates, was named to the ALA/Association of Library Trustees and Advocates National Advocacy Honor Roll in 2000, and is a former trustee of the Johnson County (Kansas) Library.